# fast coaching

# fast coaching

## THE COMPLETE GUIDE TO
## *NEW CODE* CONTINUE & BEGIN

### NICK DRAKE-KNIGHT

d

PIP
POLLINGER IN PRINT
Pollinger Limited
9 Staple Inn
Holborn
LONDON
WC1V 7QH
www.pollingerltd.com

First Published in 2016 by Pollinger in Print, an imprint of Pollinger
Limited, Drury House, 34–43 Russell Street, London WC2B 5HA.

ISBN 978-1-905665-78-5

Designed and set by seagulls.net

Cover design by Two Associates

Illustrations by Rupert Besley

Printed and bound in Great Britain by Lightning Source

*For my beautiful Clairabelle. I miss you.*

# contents

ACKNOWLEDGEMENTS                                                    ix

FOREWORD *by Zoryna O'Donnell and Simon Parrott/John Pitts*        xi

ABOUT THE AUTHOR                                                    xv

INTRODUCTION                                                         1

**Part 1**  Continue & Begin Principles                             9

**Part 2**  How to Use *Fast Coaching*                             75

**Part 3**  *New Code* Continue & Begin                           175
            – the Question Sets

**Part 4**  Coaching Session Transcripts                          185

## Appendices
Appendix 1 – Example Action Plans                                 261
Appendix 2 – Sources of Influence                                 271
Appendix 3 – Train the Trainer (TTT) programme                   275
Appendix 4 – Testimonials                                         277

FURTHER READING                                                   280

# ACKNOWLEDGEMENTS

My thanks are due to some fabulous people for their advice, encouragement and – on occasions – well-deserved criticism.

Alphabetical order is as good a sequence to follow as any, so thank you Rupert Besley for his great fun and pithy illustrations; Esther Booth for helping me better understand the realities of providing healthcare support for babies and young mums; Becky Braund for explaining the practicalities of family support work and social care; Lynne Churchill-Slough for insights into coaching potential in education (still shamefully under employed, by the way); Carol Lee for editing and unscrambling tortuous syntax into something readable; Max Fletcher for sharing his experiences of rugby coaching; Katy Loffman at Pollinger for her continuing encouragement and making things happen; Zoryna O'Donnell for her wonderful support and belief in Continue & Begin Fast Coaching as an aid to community development; Anya Penny for having the strength of character to endure hours of my face and voice in transcribing video footage.

Finally my thanks to the thousands of coaches and coachees, and trainers and trainees who have helped shape *Fast Coaching* from the first stirrings of mandatory celebration in room C46a of the Management and Business Studies Department at Isle of Wight College in 1990.

Thanks everyone.

# foreword

Coaching is well recognised as a powerful way to achieve our best, whether we focus on our personal life or career ambitions. It is also one of the most cost-effective and efficient ways to initiate and to sustain positive behavioural changes and to improve relationships with friends, family and colleagues. Over the past 25 years I have used a number of coaching models and techniques, and Continue & Begin Fast Coaching is my favourite by far.

From 2012–2015, I led on the implementation of the Strengthening Families Programme on the Isle of Wight, which gave me an opportunity to gain considerable first-hand experience of the flexibility and effectiveness of Continue & Begin Fast Coaching when working with individuals and whole family groups in challenging circumstances. The families we supported had problems with children's school attendance, offending behaviour and worklessness. Many of them also suffered from the impact of domestic abuse, substance misuse, mental health problems, poverty, debt and low aspirations. They were in and out of the public services system, struggling from one crisis to another – some for several generations. Traditional methods and interventions seem to be unable to break this vicious cycle. We needed something new, a different approach to working with those families, so we got in touch with Nick Drake-Knight.

Nick worked with my team to adapt Continue & Begin Fast Coaching for work with families and then trained us to use this technique. My colleagues and I were impressed with the speed and the impact of Continue

& Begin Fast Coaching. By using this technique, we were able to break the barriers, build rapport and facilitate sustainable positive changes in the lives of our clients: children, young people and adults – whole families.

We met the improvement target set for the Strengthening Families Programme and 65 per cent of our client families who completed their 'exit questionnaires' reported that they felt confident to continue improving, even without the involvement of our service. They commented that that our service 'helps making the family work together'. The Ofsted Inspection Report published in November 2014 also acknowledged that '... the Strengthening Families team (Troubled Families) is successfully helping children and their families to make positive changes'. I am confident that the use of Continue & Begin Fast Coaching by my team made a significant contribution to this success and helped to improve the lives of hundreds of families on the Isle of Wight and beyond.

For me, the beauty of Continue & Begin Fast Coaching is that it is 'content-free', flexible and adaptable for practically any context or circumstances. For example, I also successfully used this model in career coaching and personal performance coaching.

*Fast Coaching* is a great way to start learning this excellent coaching model. But don't stop on the book – go on the Continue & Begin Fast Coaching training course and be part of the world of coaching excellence that changes lives.

**Zoryna O'Donnell, Director of L&M Plus Consulting Ltd.**

Here at Volvo much of our success depends on us bringing new and improved models to market. Yet, as long-term users of Continue & Begin, we never felt the need to call Nick and ask when the updated version would come out. Indeed, why would we? The model worked in our world, so why change it?

It's only when you fully understand *New Code* Continue & Begin do you realise why and how it really makes the difference between good intentions and action. *New Code* has retained all those great features that attracted us to Continue & Begin in the first place: it's practical, fast and simple to communicate (as long as you have explicit standards in place!)

So what is it about *New Code* that makes a good model even better? The highlights for us are:

- more words and phrases to help get the most out of *continue to* and *begin to* principles;
- use of *Clean Language* – as Nick loves to remind us: English is Rubbish;
- greater focus on the Emotional Drivers to change;
- the power of Can't to Can Belief Busting;
- making it memorable – three chunks and seven questions;
- how to *nudge* towards those crucial explicit standards.

We've added our own good practice to *New Code* Continue & Begin by introducing post-workshop webinars. During these, three or four managers spend a quality hour on the phone with the coach, discussing the learning that has dropped out of recent C & B sessions with their team. They learn from each other, while continuing to reflect on their own coaching abilities in a positive, Continue & Begin-type manner.

What makes these sessions even more satisfying is hearing the managers (who are also mums and dads, sons and sisters, friends and colleagues) tell stories of how, as practitioners of Continue to & Begin coaching skills, they have made a real, positive difference in their personal – as well as their professional – lives.

Nick gives a great definition in the book explaining the difference between motivation and movement; after reading this book you will be motivated to use *New Code*.

**John Pitts and Simon Parrott, People and Process Development, Volvo Car UK**

# about the author

Nick Drake-Knight has a colourful career history. He started out as a 'midshipman' navigating deck cadet in the merchant navy before four years as a police officer in Bristol. Leisure industry management followed and a first taste of people development: training and coaching employees to offer outstanding service experience to customers.

By 1990 Nick was a further education lecturer, helping his mature students gain management qualifications and win regional and national awards with his innovative approach to learning and personal growth. His creative and confidence-boosting method of (what became) Continue & Begin Fast Coaching had its early successes during tutorials with student managers.

Consulting work followed, supporting business leaders to stimulate economic development in the UK, in France, and extensively in the former Eastern Bloc; East Germany, Poland and Slovakia.

He returned to the UK in 1998 as business adviser, senior adviser and later board member of the UK's largest Business Link operator, Business Link Wessex. Then for 12 years from 2002, Nick was a board director of the UK's leading multi-media mystery shopping agency.

Since 2014 he has focused exclusively on his own consultancy, in commercial and public sectors, which continues to flourish

Nick has advised world-class commercial brands including: Amer Sports, Arc'teryx, Audi, Bang & Olufsen, Barclays, B&Q, Carphone Warehouse, Fat Face, General Motors, HBOS, Harveys Furniture, Hays Travel, Heal's, Homebase, Honda, Jaguar, Kawasaki, Kia, Mazda, The Mailbox, McKinsey &

Co., Mercedes-Benz, Mitsubishi, Moss Bros, Oakley, O2, Peugeot, ProTyre, Salomon, Shell, Sports Direct, Subaru, Virgin Media, Volvo, Volkswagen and numerous SMEs (small and medium-sized enterprises) in the UK and EMEA (Europe, Middle East and Africa), including emerging economies in the former East Germany, Poland, Slovakia, Turkey and Bahrain.

Public sector clients include the Houses of Parliament, government agencies, NHS Trusts, Public Health England agencies, Housing Associations, Youth Offending Teams, Local Authorities, Education Authorities and SME economic development agencies in the UK, Eastern Europe and the Middle East.

Nick is an authority on personal development and continuous improvement. He helps global brands implement day-to-day employee development strategies. Increasingly his coaching work is used in family dynamics and social care arenas, including the UK Government's public health programme integrating healthcare and social care in the community.

He is an international conference speaker, learning and development (L&D) consultant and an experienced individual and team coach.

Nick lives by the sea on the Isle of Wight on the southern coast of England. He is a retired amateur rugby player and is, without doubt, the worst surfer in Britain.

# OTHER NDK BOOKS

*BOOMERANG! Coach Your Team to Be The Best!* 254pp., Pollinger, 2007
ISBN 978-1-905665-51-8

*MEERKAT SELLING: Be the Best in Big Ticket Retail Selling,* 206pp.,
Pollinger, 2008
ISBN 978-1-905665-70-9

*SALES HYPNOSIS: Indirect Suggestion in Sales,* 224pp., Continue &
Begin Ltd, 2004
ISBN 0-9546744-0-5

# PROFESSIONAL JOURNALS

*Journal of Customer & Contact Centre Management*
(Vol 1, Issue 2, March 2011)
'How to create a consistent and sustainable customer experience in
today's contact centre.'

*Journal of Training & Management Development Methods*
(Issue 3, Volume May 2012)
'Coaching can boost the effectiveness of sales training.' DOI 10.1108/
09513501211200811

*Journal of Training & Management Development Methods*
(Volume 26, Number 1, February 2012)
'Creating a consistent and sustainable customer experience in retail
networks.'

*Human Resource Management International Digest*
(Volume 20, Number 1, 2012)
'Training and coaching boost performance of sales staff at B&Q.'

# introduction

When I first pulled together a working version of Continue & Begin Fast Coaching back in the early 90s I had no idea I was creating a fast coaching method that would benefit so many people in such a diverse range of sectors – and in so many languages!

Continue & Begin first emerged in a further education environment, presented as an explicit model of how to strengthen ego and belief systems in adult management students. It enhanced self-worth and stimulated personal belief in opportunity and possibility. It proved remarkably effective.

a flexible model . . .

I went on to use the method in the former Soviet Union, to help managers new to free enterprise develop their competences. Subsequently it was used with owners/managers of SMEs in the UK, encouraging them to broaden their knowledge and skills in running their businesses.

Since those early days Continue & Begin has evolved into a rapid-results change tool for individuals and groups in diverse environments. It is used in business, in social and healthcare environments, in education and in the family. Thousands of Continue & Begin fast coaches now help others identify choice options, thereby developing their potential.

Continue & Begin Fast Coaching experienced a boost in popularity with the publication of my book *Boomerang! Coach Your Team to Be the Best* in 2007, which used customer service as a reference point. Of course, Continue & Begin is now used in wider settings. The common thread is the 'content-free' nature of the approach. Continue & Begin Fast Coaching remains a powerful methodology and is simple to apply.

The Continue & Begin Fast Coaching framework may be applied universally, irrespective of context. This book provides the framework model; your circumstances and context provide the content.

## *New Code* vs *Old Code* – Continue & Begin Fast Coaching

Over the years I have continued to fine-tune the model, ensuring Continue & Begin evolves as a powerful, feel-good inducing fast coaching method.

*Old Code* has done a fine job, it's now time to move over and make room for *New Code* Continue & Begin Fast Coaching. *New Code* includes elements of my own delivery patterns drawn from decades of studying with masters of personal change, including Frank Farrelly, Avy Joseph, Richard Bandler, John Grinder, Tony Robbins and most recently the amazing people at Esalen Institute in Big Sur, California.

Throughout Continue & Begin Fast Coaching the influences of Fritz Perls, Alfred Korzybski, Noam Chomsky and Milton Erickson continue to shine, especially for folk who understand the nature of their work.

*New Code* goes to the next stage in efficacy: greater emphasis on 'feeling' (an evolution of leverage), future orientation (with key questions for the coachee), implementation strategies, and insights for the coach into why basic principles from Transformational Grammar offer assistance.

When these critical elements are woven into Continue & Begin Fast Coaching in a form that is simple to understand and easy to apply, we have a new generation of fast coaching just waiting to help people celebrate and feel good and then work towards fulfilling their dreams, whatever the context.

*Old Code* is good; *New Code* is where the new thinking excites and delivers even better results.

In reviewing the inevitable evolution of Continue & Begin Fast Coaching, since the publication back in 2007 of *Boomerang!* it is clear there have been improvements woven into my own delivery style. In effect, the 'NDK style' incorporates significantly more than the *Old Code* skeleton. My intention in this book is to codify key elements of my delivery in an amended explicit model for others to choose to use, or choose to not use. *Old Code* still represents good value; it's just that it offers an impoverished representation of the full richness of Continue & Begin available to coaching professionals.

This book presents the latest evolution of Continue & Begin Fast Coaching in an easy-to-absorb format in four parts, which may appeal to different readers:

# PART 1
## Continue & Begin Principles

Part 1 explains the thinking behind Continue & Begin Fast Coaching and its *New Code* variant, why it works and how the simplicity of the model hides a sophisticated set of well-proven psychological and linguistic personal development principles. Students of linguistics and personal change will find a rich source of material here.

This section is quite technical in elements. Learning included in Part 1 offers additional insights and underpinning knowledge for the Continue & Begin fast coach who wishes to gain a deeper understanding of why Continue & Begin Fast Coaching works so well. It also offers advanced techniques for greater elegance than is offered by the basic Continue and Begin Ltd Certified Coach 1-day training course. Licensed trainers of Continue & Begin, accredited by Continue and Begin Ltd, will find the content particularly value-adding; helpful additional reference material is included to enhance and enrich training delivery.

Licensed Trainer (Train the Trainer programmes via Continue and Begin Ltd) includes elements of this material to strengthen underpinning knowledge and understanding for new trainers of the Certified Coach 1-day programme.

Not all the learning content in Part 1 is necessarily essential for a Continue & Begin Certified Coach to operate effectively. Practitioners who simply wish to use and enjoy the impact of *New Code* Continue & Begin Fast Coaching in its base format can do so, comfortable in the knowledge that solid principles and methodologies are at the foundation of their personal fast coaching effectiveness.

# PART 2
## How to Use *Fast Coaching*

Part 2 presents bite-sized learning points comprising content from a series of *New Code* training presentations, delivered by Continue and Begin Ltd.

Readers will experience the core messages and principal learning points in a cogent sequence.

Guided learning transcripts are sourced from a series of video presentations recorded in 2014 and 2015. The transcripts are copied verbatim from the film clips, so expect 'spoken' English, with colloquialisms, idioms and the shortcuts on grammar you may typically hear when someone speaks rather than writes. As well as being informative, it's a fun read!

The hypnotherapist Milton Erickson would say to his patients, 'My voice will go with you'. If it is helpful, you may wish to 'prime' your mind by listening to my voice and experiencing my non-verbal communication and mannerisms via www.continueandbegin.com or at the Nick Drake-Knight channel on YouTube https://www.youtube.com/user/NDKgroup before reading this book.

# PART 3
## *New Code* Continue & Begin – The Question Sets

This part presents a simple flow through the core question steps in *New Code* and Can't to Can Belief Busting. If you'd like to skip straight to the models themselves, this is the section for you. It's concise, targeted and presents the core questions used in these fast-acting approaches to people change.

Take note though, elegance comes from a deeper underpinning knowledge and understanding, not simple replication of a set of questions or parrot-fashion mimicking. It's great to use Continue & Begin; it's even more rewarding when you understand how it works. Part 1 and Part 2 lead the reader towards a heightened awareness.

# PART 4
## Coaching Session Transcripts

Examples of *New Code* Continue & Begin Fast Coaching and Can't to Can Belief Busting sessions are transcribed into written format in Part 4. These illustrations provide an insight into an effective application of *New Code* across a range of environments, including education, family work, housing and care, business and healthcare.

Students of 'pattern' will find these transcripts particularly useful as each example provides written evidence of a design configuration (the Continue & Begin model) being followed by the coach.

I hope you enjoy this book, that you find it informative, and go on to use *Fast Coaching* to help people celebrate their successes, feel good about themselves and subsequently further develop their talents, whether at work, in education, in a family, or in the wider community.

*Nick Drake-Knight*
*Cliff Cottages*
*Isle of Wight*
*2016*

Train the Trainer programmes are available via Continue and Begin Ltd to transfer *New Code* Continue & Begin training technology in a quality assured format.

Direct delivery of Continue & Begin training (Certified Coach and Licensed Trainer) by Continue and Begin Ltd is available via www.continueandbegin.com

Video examples of Nick Drake-Knight using Continue & Begin Fast Coaching to develop individuals are available at www.continueandbegin.com and via the Nick Drake-Knight channel on YouTube https://www.youtube.com/user/NDKgroup

# PART I

## continue & begin principles

# Continue & Begin Fast Coaching
## – What Is It?

Continue & Begin Fast Coaching is a personal development framework that helps individuals and groups grow skills and competences. It creates rapid change in personal behaviour. Continue & Begin is used in business, education, families and communities to help people achieve their personal development ambitions, built on confidence gained from recognising their existing competences.

Continue & Begin promotes positivity by celebrating personal successes and strengthening ego, before considering opportunities to operate differently, or even better.

It is a well-proven technique that builds capability, capacity and consequently enhances performance. Continue & Begin is now used as the preferred people development model in a diverse range of environments including business, education establishments, healthcare operations and family contexts.

It is not necessary to become a qualified coach to help people. By using Continue & Begin as the agent of change we can create significant shifts in a person's professional or personal life. Because of its focus on ego-strengthening it is safe to use, even in the clumsiest of hands.

Continue & Begin Fast Coaching can be used to help children at school, or to develop an employee's skills in the workplace, to encourage an individual's healthy living and well-being or to support families in need of a helping hand. It has no boundaries for its application.

Key to the success of Continue & Begin is the speed of its application and its positive impact on ego. Unlike many coaching models, Continue & Begin is quick to use and can be successfully applied to an individual seeking help (the coachee) in a few minutes.

A core skill of an effective Continue & Begin coach is to make careful use of language during the coaching process. Continue & Begin promotes specific language patterns as helpful in the coaching process, and identifies key phrases and patterns as less helpful.

# Origins of Continue & Begin
# Fast Coaching

I developed Continue & Begin when lecturing mature students in management studies. One-to-one tutorials were enlightening. I found to my surprise even the most self-assured, assertive and apparently confident managers harboured anxieties and self-doubt about personal performance and capability. I discovered that only a few of my students were skilled at celebrating their successes.

For many, their critical inner voice was hard at work undermining their achievements and skills, suggesting frailties hidden from others, and re-running internal videos and audio tapes of things they wish they had said and done at work and things they wished they *hadn't* said and done. 'What other people think' was a thread through much of their internal processing. Many of my students were outstanding at personal criticism. I clearly remember during coursework assessment giving one manager a 'Distinction for Self-Flagellation'.

Trust began to build between tutor and student. Managers' personal masks fell away and the real person emerged. Tutorials became honest and hidden anxieties surfaced. 'What if I fail?' and 'I can't do this' were phrases I heard often.

I encountered managers who were clearly under enormous personal pressure: in responsible managerial roles during difficult economic times. Many students had the additional burden of organisations that dwelled on improvement needs, with minimal recognition of continuing successful performance. The financial well-being of their family unit depended on success at work. It was a potent mix: strain at work, money worries, balancing home life, child care, and relationships – and now a professional development management course!

I determined to embark on a programme of ego-strengthening. The origins of my strategy lay in therapeutic work I was studying at the time. I began each tutorial with *enforced celebration*. I asked each management student to highlight their professional and personal achievements since our last tutorial and to make a note of these successes. I was ruthless in demanding adherence to celebration. The effect was dramatic. Students' physiology changed; their facial expressions, posture, breathing patterns, minor motor movements, skin tone and language patterns all changed as they began to acknowledge their achievements and recognise how talented they were.

For some, we considered 'What would happen if?' and an early version of Can't to Can Belief Busting evolved. For others, we explored what eventually became known as their Structure of Well-Done-Ness.

Confidence was manifest! Students began to think of professional development built on a platform of personal confidence. Grades improved. We won awards. We were onto something.

## Good and Less Good

In the 1990s I worked as a consultant in what used to be known as the Eastern Bloc, or former Soviet Union, in Poland, Slovakia and the former East Germany. Amongst other projects, I helped managers of former communist state-run enterprises to understand a new free market economy, where consumer demand was king. The Soviet centralised economy and mass distribution no longer existed. I worked through an intermediary, Mariusz, a young graduate of Poznan University. Mariusz was in his early twenties, full of energy and optimism. He embraced the new capitalism with relish and boundless enthusiasm.

Our first assignment was in Kalisz in south west Poland, west of Lodz. We were to run a business seminar the following day for senior managers from the local area (Voivodeship). We were at his dacha – a kind of wooden shack on a piece of land outside the city – drinking vodka and eating local Polish food on a barbeque. We chatted about the adventure ahead.

'Mariusz, how many of the managers tomorrow can speak English?'
'Some of them,' Mariusz said, '… their English is good. And some of them … their English is less good.'

The next day I met the managers and we explored business ideas. I could just about converse with those whose English was *good*. The managers with *less good* English? Well, my Polish was better than their English. *Taka prawda!*

Mariusz habitually used this language pattern, 'X positive' and 'X less positive'. It was a pattern that repeated in his communication. For Mariusz, things were good and less good, talented and less talented, skilful and less skilful, beautiful and less beautiful, good value or less good value. There was no 'bad' for Mariusz – only 'less good'.

I was impressed by his mindset. A young man was teaching an older man a productive way of thinking. This was a positive and healthy model of self-talk, what Epictetus called 'judgement on events' (framing) and much later, Aaron Beck's encouragement for us to 'reframe' negative circumstances.

*Good* and *less good* began to fit with my early shaping of Continue & Begin Fast Coaching. Today, for Continue & Begin coaches, reflecting on *good* is helpful for *nudging* the coachee (more on *nudging* later) towards recognition of successful performance.

Identifying *less good* behaviours is a smart move for *nudging* the coachee towards the most value-adding *begin to* behaviours.

So, thank you Mariusz for the learning. Oh, and the vodka too. *Na zdrowie!*

## Patterns Which Connect

I have admiration for the biologist, anthropologist, cyberneticist and ecologist Gregory Bateson (1904–1980).

I discovered Bateson's work in the early 90s when I first read *Structure of Magic (Volume 1)*, Richard Bandler and John Grinder's first text about what, in the 1970s when the book was written, was called META, later evolving into what became known as neuro-linguistic programming (NLP). Bandler and Grinder's book described the linguistic patterns found from modelling world-renowned experts in human communication and change, including the originator of gestalt therapy Fritz Perls, family therapist Virginia Satir and hypnotherapist Milton Erickson.

Bateson had been a significant influence on Bandler and Grinder's work. He offered access to an impressive network of contacts and stimulating ideas. I have a keen interest in 'the source of the sauce' and wanted to know more about Bateson.

Here was a man who was a true polymath, that is, an expert in many different fields of endeavour. He started out as a biologist, then became an anthropologist and evolved into a thinker, researcher and commentator on a diverse range of disciplines including psychology, systems thinking and cybernetics, ecological integrity and environmentalism.

His concept of *mind* in nature was fascinating – the idea that an ecological collective of animals, plants and an eco-system could adapt to an environment. He referred to a *mind* as '… an aggregate of interacting parts or components'.

The most intriguing of all Bateson's ideas was his reference to what he called *patterns which connect*. He highlighted how patterns in nature are repeated in diverse sets of animals, plants and organisms. He identified patterns that connect in language, in communities and in communication. He proposed that connectivity and patterns are everywhere. Continue & Begin Fast Coaching is one such pattern that connects.

Continue & Begin is what Milton Erickson called 'content-free', that is, there is no specific situational message. It is a framework that can be applied in a diverse range of circumstances with an equally diverse range of 'players'. The beauty of Continue & Begin is the emphasis on ego-strengthening, the celebration of success (no matter how small) and the stimulation of a renewed confidence to take on fresh *begin to* challenges. It doesn't matter what the context is, or the subjective content, or who the individual coachee is.

Continue & Begin Fast Coaching is now used in commercial and public sector business, in family support agencies, in care and support organisations, in housing, in sport and in education. It is what Gregory Bateson referred to as a *pattern which connects*.

# Criticism and Change

When we focus on what's wrong in our lives we shut out positivity and opportunity. Transfer this reality to the world of coaching others and we create stunted thinking and limited possibilities.

Recent research analysing brain-imaging patterns highlights how important it is to think productively about potential outcomes rather than current limitations. This is the essence of Continue & Begin Fast Coaching.

A group of researchers at Case Western Reserve University, in Cleveland, Ohio, examined the effects of a 30-minute coaching session focusing on positive emotional attractors (PEA), and a second 30-minute session focusing on negative emotional attractors (NEA) (Boyatzis, Jack, Cesaro, Passarelli and Khawaja, 2010).

Respondents talked about their dreamed-about future ten years ahead (the PEA coaching), activating parts of the visual cortex involved in imagining things. The positive interview elicited feelings of pleasure, hope and inspiration. Meanwhile, the NEA session, which asked students about how they were doing on their homework, readings and assignments, revealed such questioning activated areas known to indicate anxiety, self-consciousness and guilt. Performance anxiety is well known in therapeutic circles as a (common) inhibitor of well-being and consequently, achievement.

Boyatzis recognises the dangers of what I call *failure focus.*

Another implication is that … a focus on what needs to be fixed, and overcoming weaknesses and 'gaps' has the exact opposite effect on the subject of the interview. The discussion only cements the subject's defensiveness and potential to discount any benefit of the recommendations or advice. While it may invoke compliance-oriented behavior, any positive effect of such activities or desire for improvement will probably be short-lived.

Boyatzis commented,

Our results suggest that engaging in a performance review ...
is quite different than engaging someone in a developmental
discussion. The more evaluating ... discussion actually leads a
person to be more neurologically closed to new ideas or to work on
learning or changing.

In 'The Neurochemistry of Positive Conversations', (*Harvard Business Review*, June 2014) Judith and Richard Glaser explore the hormones produced in our bodies when stimulated by 'the chemistry of conversations'.

When we face criticism, rejection or fear, when we feel marginalized
or minimized, our bodies produce higher levels of cortisol, a hormone
that shuts down the thinking center of our brains and activates
conflict aversion and protection behaviors. We become more
reactive and sensitive. We often perceive even greater judgment and
negativity than actually exists. And these effects can last for 26 hours
or more, imprinting the interaction on our memories and magnifying
the impact it has on our future behavior. Cortisol functions like a
sustained-release tablet – the more we ruminate about our fear, the
longer the impact.

Positive comments and conversations produce a chemical
reaction too. They spur the production of oxytocin, a feel-good
hormone that elevates our ability to communicate, collaborate and
trust others by activating networks in our prefrontal cortex. But
oxytocin metabolizes more quickly than cortisol, so its effects are less
dramatic and long-lasting.

In Continue & Begin Fast Coaching we help people self-identify successes and build ego, empowering coachees with sufficient self-confidence to take on personal development goals with enthusiasm and optimism. Maybe without even knowing, Continue & Begin Fast Coaching has been stimulating oxytocin production for years!

# Why is Continue & Begin Different, Specifically?

Five reasons:

1. ## Continue & Begin is *fast!*

   This is a far quicker coaching approach than most 'established' methodologies. Many coaching methods require anything from 20 minutes to over an hour to create a meaningful change plan for an individual coachee. With Continue & Begin we can achieve substantial impact in less than 2 minutes and a really comprehensive change strategy within 6 or 7 minutes, depending on environment and the complexity of the coachee's ambition.

2. ## Continue & Begin makes people *feel good*

   An individual is more likely to take on fresh challenges and new goals when in a state of confidence and personal feel-good. The starting point for a successful Continue & Begin Fast Coaching session is to focus on the coachee's recent successes and a celebration of performance as measured against previously agreed standards, rules or ambitions.

   By emphasising existing competence and capability, the coachee is stimulated to recognise self-worth and self-image, enhancing ego and personal confidence. By contrast, a person with impoverished self-perception is less likely to feel confident, capable or willing to take on further 'stretch'.

3. ## It is a *content-free* model

   There is no industry or environment-specific jargon or set of references. Continue & Begin Fast Coaching can be used in a diverse range of circumstances. Because it's so flexible there are few, if any, scenarios where a coachee cannot be helped to further his or her competency through the application of a Continue & Begin approach. The core framework remains the same, whatever the environment.

4. **Language patterns are carefully crafted**

   *Specificity questions* elicit responses that aid the coachee in achieving her ambitions. Proven patterning from transformational grammar and NLP release potential in the coachee and stimulate personal growth.

5. ***New Code* Continue & Begin Fast Coaching is here!**

   *New Code* is an evolution of the original fast coaching model first designed in the 1990s. It includes specific reference to *future feeling* and how identification of an Emotional Driver can create psychological leverage for action. This is a key development in the model and one that radically increases commitment to change and practical activity. *New Code* includes enhanced understanding about the dangers of *surface structure utterance, deletion, distortion* and *generalisation* statements, how these can be identified and what questioning strategies can be used to establish greater specificity in communication for the coachee. Add to that an increased emphasis on implementation strategy and we have a step change from the original model.

## How does *New Code* Continue & Begin Fast Coaching Work?

That's what this book is about!

Most coaching methods begin with a stated goal or ambition identified by the coachee, or in some cases identified (or imposed) by the coach. There is an immediate and stated focus on improvement. Too often there is an implication from the coach, or inference taken by the coachee, that current performance or behaviour is not satisfactory. There is a presupposition inherent in coaching processes that suggests criticism and accusations of inadequacy.

Continue & Begin starts with celebration – of existing skills, achievements and successes. These are known as *continue to* behaviours and constitute the building blocks towards personal confidence, so important in preparing the coachee for further personal development.

In Continue & Begin we place great emphasis on securing self-identified successes, no matter how small or insignificant they may seem. Many individuals find it troublesome to self-identify personal excellence: they are concerned they may be considered as boasting or arrogant. Sometimes teasing out recognition of personal success is a major task. Continue & Begin coaches learn the art of *nudging*, to help an individual verbalise an attribute the coach has already identified through observation.

## Continue to ...

For *continue to* behaviours to have optimum effect in boosting ego they are best related to a set of pre-determined *standards, rules* or *ambitions*. These criteria will differ depending on context, for (random) example:

**Business**
- Technical operating principles
- Compliance with explicitly described employment contract requirements
- Call centre processes
- Customer service procedures
- Sales behaviour patterns.

**Education**
- Coursework assignment criteria
- Performance against syllabus requirements

- Compliance with institutional rules
- Time management expectations.

**Health and well-being**
- Previously agreed (explicitly described) healthy-eating goals
- Exercise schedules
- Healthy-living strategies
- Rehabilitation plans.

**Family**
- Contributing to identified family chores
- Supportive and nurturing communication towards other family members
- Compliance with previously determined family rules or values
- Implementing responsibility for personal behaviour (specific references required).

By identifying a set of productive, positive behaviours exhibited by the coachee that relate to a given set of known *standards,* we can help the individual celebrate her existing or evolving excellence. By doing so we can build an ego strong enough for the coachee to take on further personal development ambitions in the form of *begin to* commitments.

As we progress through this book it will become clear why it is essential that *continue to* behaviours are self-identified by the coachee, rather than being told by the coach.

This is a key differential and is at the core of Continue & Begin Fast Coaching. It is imperative the coachee is empowered by self-reflection on her existing prowess. Our goal as Continue & Begin practitioners is to arouse a strong psychological sense of resourcefulness and confidence in the subject before she embarks on plans for improvement.

## Begin to ...
*Begin to* behaviours are developmental. In many coaching methodologies this is (wrongly) the starting point. In Continue & Begin we don't even

consider improvement, self-development or remedial work until a set of *continue to* successes have been loudly hailed and celebrated, thereby strengthening the individual's self-perception.

Once we have a coachee sufficiently confident we can activate the *begin to* phase with a small set of targeted, specific ambitions. The number of *begin to* behaviours identified and committed to are deliberately kept to a modest number – a maximum of three ambitions for change, in many cases just one or two.

The rationale for this is based on short-term memory capacity and the ability of individuals to consciously consider new ideas during 'performance'. Therapists understand performance anxiety is exacerbated by overload. Later in this book we explore the research of George Miller, who identified limiting factors in short-term memory and conscious thinking.

In Continue & Begin we ask the coachee to focus on just a few new ways of operating within their personal development plan. Critically, if a personal development plan is to concentrate on just a few new behaviours, it makes sense for those ambitions to be significant and value-adding, not trivial or marginal in benefit. So, although only a few *begin to* behaviours are identified and committed to by the coachee, a high-impact set of *begin to* goals will be capacity building and therefore valuable.

## Ratio of *Continue to* versus *Begin to* Behaviours

Community members across many cultures have been conditioned to expect criticism and demands for continuous improvement in whatever field of endeavour they operate. By contrast, the starting point for Continue & Begin is to strengthen ego in the coachee by celebrating personal successes. To achieve this, Continue & Begin seeks to identify twice as many *continue to* behaviours as *begin to* commitments.

In circumstances where evidence of performance is in abundance, it may be possible to achieve an action plan of x6 *continue to* behaviours and x3 *begin to* commitments (in Continue & Begin parlance, a '6 & 3').

In other contexts and scenarios it may be 4 & 2, or in some cases 2 & 1, depending on the complexity of circumstance and context.

A strict 2:1 ratio is not necessary however, as long as identified *continue to* successes significantly outnumber the *begin to* development plans. A good action plan may be a 5 & 3, a 3 & 2 or a 4 & 1. The key is emphasis on celebration, leading to confidence, leading to ambitions for personal development.

## In What Circumstances Is Continue & Begin Fast Coaching Best Used?

There are three typical 'channels' of use for Continue & Begin:

Reflective Behaviour

1. Reflective behaviour – where an individual is encouraged to reflect on recent performance at work, at school, in sports, in personal healthcare or at home in the family unit. The Continue & Begin coach will use carefully crafted questions to help a coachee reflect and consider the successful specific behaviours she would like to *continue to* do well, and to agree on a limited number of behaviours the coachee would like to *begin to* do differently – perhaps even better.

## Observed Behaviour

2. **Observed behaviour** – where an individual is observed and listened to 'in action' and is then fast-coached by the observing practitioner using prompts, questions and non-verbal communication contained within the Continue & Begin model. The coachee is asked to consider her performance (as observed by the coach) and to identify *continue to* and *begin to* behaviours while the recent performance experience is still fresh in the memory. This is referred to by some practitioners of Continue & Begin as *in-the-moment* coaching.

3. **Recorded behaviour** – where an individual's performance has been recorded on film, on audio file or in written form. In business environments these will typically include overt filming, covert mystery shop recordings, call centre telephone recordings, written or design work, or email communication. In sports, the arts or social environments recorded behaviour will often include video footage or audio recordings of personal performance. In education this may include assignment work or written study submissions.

A common theme in all three of these channels of use is self-evaluation of personal performance by the coachee, guided by the Continue & Begin practitioner. Evaluation is carried out as measurement against a given of

Recorded Behaviour

standards, rules, values or ambitions previously determined and made explicit.

*Note: Assessment is difficult unless the process includes a comparison of performance against an explicitly described set of expectations.*

## Explicitly Described Performance Expectations

Coaching works best when an individual coachee – or a collective group of coachees – reflect on their recent, current and planned future activity. Reflection includes an assessment against a set of previously agreed behaviours, performance criteria or personal expectations of self.

In my book *Boomerang!* – and in numerous publications, conference events and trainings – I have referred to a Model of Excellence as a means of representing the essential need for a set of criteria for a coachee/individual to assess themselves against in order to leverage personal change. This was – and is – particularly relevant to the commercial world.

**The Model of Excellence**

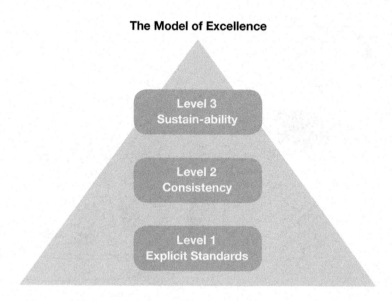

## Level 1 – Explicit standards

Leading operators have an explicit set of performance standards spelling out exactly what is expected of employees. This approach applies irrespective of the discipline, industry sector or activity. People need to know what is expected of them if they are to work to a given standard.

## Level 2 – Consistency

Top-performing organisations strive for consistency of excellence in all geographic and functional areas. Effective training can help with this, especially when it is practically (competence) based and aligned with the explicit standards of performance prescribed by the business.

But here's the rub: consistency is of limited value if it's temporary. World-class operators know that performance excellence must be delivered day in and day out, long after the latest training initiative has been launched. In some organisations, training is like throwing wet mud against the wall: most of the mud slides off the wall immediately.

## Level 3 – Sustainability

In fact, training is a complete waste of energy and resources unless it is made *sustainable*.

Key to sustainability is the development of a coaching philosophy and skill set that allows local managers to keep the plates spinning long after the training event has passed. Sustainability through local coaching and management keeps the momentum up and the training alive!

## Explicit Standards – at Work and Beyond

The more I used Continue & Begin in non-organisational contexts (i.e. environments that are not already 'organised'), the more I recognised the variability of likely standards or ambitions.

It was clear that a set of explicitly described reference points are necessarily required if the coachee is to assess herself. Not having reference points makes the assessment process difficult – there is no calibration against which to evaluate personal behaviour.

It seemed to me valuable to work with the coachee to jointly develop a set of standards or ambitions, in advance of the coaching process itself.

Explicit standards exist in virtually any performance or personal behaviour scenario. For example:

- business/employment
- family
- health and well-being
- supported living
- education
- sport.

The Model of Excellence was a simple representation of what it takes to deliver sustained, consistent and high-quality performance.

Gradual evolution born of experience means change. We can now productively use a developed version of The Model of Excellence in a fresh format, expanding on typical components found within most sets of explicit standards, now known as the NDK Performance Model.

## Business/employment

In a commercial or organisational environment the NDK Performance Model works effectively as a means of identifying and illustrating the expectations placed on employees or members. It requires populating with content for it to be a useful reference for coachees.

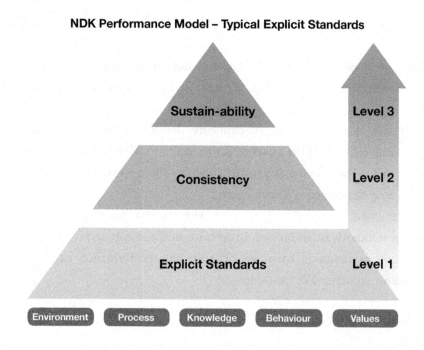

**NDK Performance Model – Typical Explicit Standards**

- **Environment** – expectations regarding maintenance of physical surroundings within which an individual operates, including how resources are to be used;

- **Process** – procedures, practices and flow of activities required to achieve success;

- **Knowledge** – an individual's underpinning knowledge and understanding required to achieve successful performance;

- **Behaviour** – expectation of personal communication, verbal and non-verbal, which contribute to effective outcomes;

- Values – where a set of organisational values or cultural expectations are in place.

## Families: ambitions, aspirations and goals

In my work within family coaching, I designed – with input from family support professionals – a revised NDK Performance Model.

**NDK Performance Model – Ambitions, Aspirations and Goals**

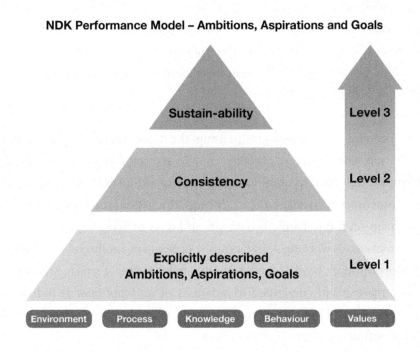

As a framework document this works fine. It is similar to the NDK Performance Model used in commercial and organisational contexts in that the framework requires to be populated with specific content. Without content it remains an interesting conceptual idea.

### Explicitly described ambitions, aspirations, goals

People are 'teleological' by nature, that is, we work most effectively when we have a goal direction. Coachees are most likely to succeed if they are clear about what they wish to achieve. A preliminary discussion around ambitions, aspirations and goals will help.

### Consistency

True success comes when new behaviours are exhibited consistently in a diverse range of environments and situations.

Consistency of new behaviour is especially important for teams, groups and families.

### Sustainability

Consistency is of limited value if it is temporary. When new behaviours are delivered – day in, day out – they become habit-ual. *New Code* Continue & Begin Fast Coaching helps people create sustain-ability, the ability to sustain.

Fast coaching of a family group using the Continue & Begin method works well when there is collective buy-in to well-formed outcomes for the family, described as ambitions, aspirations and goals. Key to achieving these outcomes is to shape them, through discussion, towards a common agreement on future family behaviours and ways of living together.

Professionals working with Continue & Begin in family contexts helped me develop the 'home' model shown below: Our Family Ambitions. Notice the explicitly described foundations of *building trust* at individual and group level. This is a prerequisite for all successful applications of *New Code* Continue & Begin Fast Coaching.

There is obvious similarity between the NDK Performance Model – Ambitions, Aspirations, Goals (AAG) – and the Our Family Ambitions format. In both illustrations the common denominators are:

1. trust-building;
2. deciding AAG;
3. implementation of new behaviours and their consistent application;
4. sustained application of new behaviours.

Both representation formats are fit for purpose.

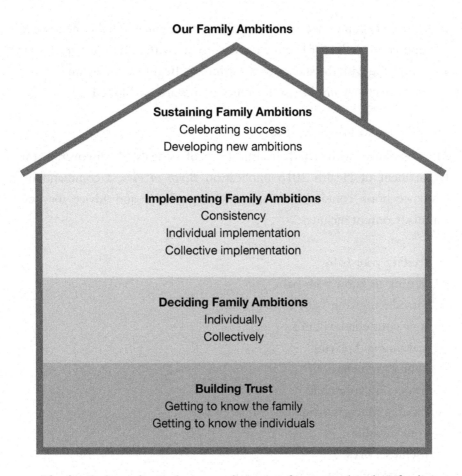

**Our Family Ambitions**

**Sustaining Family Ambitions**
Celebrating success
Developing new ambitions

**Implementing Family Ambitions**
Consistency
Individual implementation
Collective implementation

**Deciding Family Ambitions**
Individually
Collectively

**Building Trust**
Getting to know the family
Getting to know the individuals

If a family has a limited set, or absence, of organised 'rules' for living together, it is unlikely that members of the family will have a common understanding of what is expected of them, in terms of behaviour.

It therefore becomes necessary to establish those rules, whether negotiated or imposed, in order for family members to know the extent to which they are complying with the standards. Continue & Begin Fast Coaching cannot proceed effectively until these reference points are established.

## Childcare – *Birth to Five*

After working with child healthcare professionals, I discovered the Department of Health 2015 publication *Birth to Five*, a commendable reference book containing 186 pages of guidance and advice for new parents. Content includes:

- feeding your baby
- getting to know your baby
- introducing your baby to solid food
- how your child will grow
- learning and playing
- habits and behaviour
- protecting your child
- treating illnesses, infections and injuries
- your own life
- useful services
- benefits and rights in the workplace.

The challenge comes when we expect a new parent to read, digest and action the contents of this document. Not all parents will have the inclination or time to absorb the detailed content of *Birth to Five*.

What parents and healthcare professionals *do* have here is a set of good practice guidelines that can be used as a resource to help celebrate existing *continue to* behaviours and identify potential *begin to* ambitions. This is where health visitors and other professionals can help the new parents – by using Continue & Begin Fast Coaching.

Below is a set of ambitions – prepared jointly with a new mum – focusing on the important topic of preventing Sudden Infant Death Syndrome (SIDS). Good practice in relation to SIDS prevention might include the following activities, some of which have been sourced from *Birth to Five* and from www.lullabytrust.org.uk . These topics can be usefully discussed during ante natal appointments with midwife or health visitor:

- Place baby in sleep bag at sleep time;
- Place baby on his back to sleep, feet at bottom of Moses basket;
- Use a firm, flat, waterproof mattress in good condition;
- If your baby has rolled onto their tummy, turn them onto their back again;
- Once baby can roll from back to front and back again, on their own, they can be left to find their own position;
- Tuck in sheets under baby's armpits, no higher;
- Don't cover your baby's face or head while sleeping or use loose bedding;
- Keep home temperature between 18 to 20 centigrade;
- Be ready to move baby into his own cot at 6 months old;
- Avoid smoking in the home;
- Don't sleep in the same bed as baby if you smoke, drink or take drugs or if your baby was born prematurely or was of low birth weight;
- Never sleep on a sofa or in an armchair with your baby.

These are just a few reference points for the parent to consider in relation to the specific topic of SIDS.

Through Continue & Begin Fast Coaching it becomes possible for the parent to refer to these points and consider what she is already doing well (build Mum's self-image, celebrate success, feel good, confidence) and then identify one or two from the list which she will *begin to* do from now on.

Without the reference list it is almost impossible for the parent to conduct a self-assessment and consequently she becomes reliant on the healthcare professional to *tell* her what to do. One of the primary tenets of Continue & Begin Fast Coaching is that *telling* doesn't work as effectively as self-discovery and self-actualization.

## Education

In schools there is real potential to help children build self-image and confidence through Continue & Begin Fast Coaching as a means of preparing the ground for further personal development. Opportunities exist to use Continue & Begin in both academic and behavioural contexts.

Let's take the behavioural route for a moment. As with the child healthcare example above, some form of reference is required for a student to know how he is performing; that is, the standards, ambitions or expectations he can measure himself against.

The example code of conduct below comes from a (randomly selected) UK secondary school. It offers a starting point for Continue & Begin coaching. These markers can be usefully referred to when discussing behaviours with a student at the school. We can help the student celebrate examples of exemplary behaviour from this list, to build self-image and confidence.

It is expected that students will:

- move sensibly, quietly and safely around the school;
- treat each other with courtesy, respect and good manners;
- participate in all lessons and create an environment to encourage all students to learn;
- attend lessons promptly, equipped and ready to learn to the best of their ability;
- care for equipment, belongings and our environment;
- follow instructions and requests from all school staff at the first request.

To help the school ensure that bullying does not take place, all students are encouraged to:

- not allow someone to be deliberately left out of a group;
- not smile or laugh when someone is being bullied;
- tell a member of staff what is happening;
- encourage the bullied student to join in with their activities or groups;
- tell the bullying student that they disapprove of his or her actions.

As the ego builds so the student can be encouraged to celebrate his achievements and, feeling good about his ability to behave appropriately, consider how his behaviours could be developed further.

In an academic context Continue & Begin can work super-effectively. Take this set of 'good practices' jointly identified by a student and her parent:

- Keep up attendance above 95%;
- Arrive at school before 8.30;
- Submit Y10 coursework on time;
- Practise speaking French with friends, weekly;
- Read English Lit text weekly now till Easter;
- Help with choreography at Rock Challenge;
- Use Outlook diary for scheduling revision;
- Do 1 old exam paper each week until mocks;
- Diarise which subject papers when;
- Finish coursework 1 week b4 deadlines.

These ambitions set out a meaningful set of reference points for subsequent coaching, whether that is a parental activity, via a school-based development session or a peer-driven activity.

- Which ambitions does the student already achieve and pledges to *continue to*?
- Which are ambitions the student commits to *begin to* do?

Continue & Begin Fast Coaching action plans are an output from the fast coaching process, providing a written record of the *continue to*'s and *begin to*'s identified during the coaching session. Examples of action plans are provided in Appendix 1. The context or circumstances for these action plans include:

- family nurturing (Dad)
- managing domestic finances
- developing retail selling skills
- personal health and well-being

- parenting childcare (SIDS)
- retirement – making the most of leisure time
- sport – hockey team player
- housing (supported living)
- automotive sales – sales process compliance.

## Old Code vs New Code

*Old Code* Continue & Begin Fast Coaching offered an effective linguistic framework for stimulating change in a person's behaviour. It was fast and made people feel good. It was, however, an impoverished methodology. *Old Code* has built-in constraints that limit potential positive outputs.

Original *Old Code* presented a simplistic 5-step questioning model for use in rapid personal change. The questioning model was as follows:

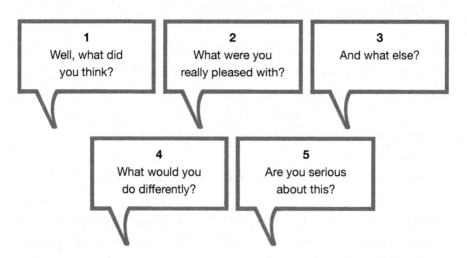

*New Code* does the same by chunking to three components:

1. CELEBRATE!
2. CHANGE!
3. COMMIT!

Each chunk contains two or three questions. The new model achieves significantly greater impact than *Old Code*, with negligible additional activity or time.

**1. *CELEBRATE!***

**2. *CHANGE!***

**3. *COMMIT!***

### *Old Code* impact

A primary measure of impact must be the implementation of committed actions over a sustained period, until the actions have become 'habit-ual' for the individual coachee or group of coachees. Too often, follow-up enquiries on Continue & Begin implementation reveal that coachees, whether individually or collectively as part of an organisation or client group, have either:

1.  partially or completely failed to implement their avowed 'action intent';

2.  applied energy in implementation of actions for a limited period of time before reverting to previously embedded behaviours and practices;

3.  behaved in a manner suggesting token application.

In essence, the Zalucki rallying cry of 'Commitment is doing the thing you said you would do, long after the mood you have said it in has left you' has not been lived up to.

So what are the reasons for these limiting factors?

## Why *Old Code* Is Impoverished

### Limited recognition of *surface structure* restrictions

Experience as a therapist and counsellor has heightened my competence in recognising and questioning a coachee's *surface structure* utterances. I intuitively use questioning techniques during the fast coaching process to explore the coachee's *deep structure* vocabulary options and thereby gain a closer understanding of true *meaning, experience* or *hallucination* in the coachee's mind.

In Continue & Begin training days and conference events I may (dependent on audience) include a brief explanation of *surface structure, deep structure* and *meaning, experience* or *hallucination*.

To date, this has not been an explicitly described component in *Old Code*.

## Limited knowledge-sharing of basic principles of Transformational Grammar

As above, understanding of restrictions in meaning accuracy caused by *deletion, distortion* and *generalisation* in communication are implicit in my personal coaching style and delivery of Continue & Begin training days and conference events.

Recognition of these restrictions in communication accuracy, and what to do about them in the form of clarifying questions, is not part of *Old Code* Continue & Begin.

## Limited recognition or application of the Emotional Driver as leverage for action

Implicit in the effectiveness of Continue & Begin and in its subset Can't to Can Belief Busting, is the importance of emotional leverage as a motivator for personal change.

*New Code* highlights the essential requirement to tie back action plan commitments to the coachee's Emotional Driver. A skilled Continue & Begin coach will ensure the coachee reflects on his/her internal motivator for implementing and making habit-ual the changes identified and committed to in the action plan.

## Limited encouragement for Future Orientation in Time

Humans are purposeful or 'teleological' in nature, that is, we operate most effectively when we have a clearly defined goal or ambition we wish to achieve. The psychologist Alfred Adler knew about this and described in his work moving from *inferiority* to *completeness*. If we consider a future time and place when we have achieved our objective(s), we can hallucinate our experience at that imaginary time, thereby releasing the 'state' feelings we associate with that future existence that we currently aspire towards.

Imagination is a powerful and influential motivator for personal action. This is a pragmatic approach already in use in therapeutic contexts. Hypnotherapists use a method known as Pseudo-Orientation in Time to help patients access an imaginary future existence, beneficial to the client's well-being.

*New Code* asks the coachee to imagine a future state and the emotions accessible at that future time. By these means we are able to mobilise the coachee's resources and get on the path to successful implementation.

## Limited emphasis on implementation strategies for *begin to* behaviours

*Old Code* simply identified what the coachee would *begin to* do. There was no mention of a *strategy* for making it happen. This left some coachees with a vague aspiration that had little – if any – precision about how it would be achieved. As a result, too many value-adding *begin to* ambitions fell by the wayside as individuals struggled with implementation.

*New Code* asks the coachee to think through *how* she will make the *begin to* happen, using a well-proven question known as a modal operator of possibility, a question form already used by Continue & Begin practitioners in the Can't to Can Belief Busting model.

## Impoverishment through 'Echo Questions'

Although the simplicity of the *Old Code* model aids replication by practitioners, this creates a tendency to repeat certain questions parrot fashion, in the form of an echo.

Specifically, 'What else (… were you pleased with)?' is an important question, teasing out a *yes set* of celebratory successes. A strength of Continue & Begin is the mandatory self-celebration, so effective in preparing the ground in readiness for *begin to* aspirations.

Limitations arise when the practitioner uses this core question repeatedly, with an exact replication, time and again. 'What else? What else? What else? What else? What else?'; it can be interrogatory and perceived as demanding – even aggressive.

It was always my intention to provide for a degree of flexibility of language within the core questions to avoid this 'machine gun' interrogation. This was not made explicit in *Old Code*. Some coaches did not/do not have adequate range in their vocabulary to achieve this flexibility and as a result stick rigidly with the same pattern.

*New Code* offers increased elasticity of language within a familiar pattern of Continue & Begin questions. Prompts are offered for practitioners to select from, enabling more variety and options for the coach. Questions are from the same family of enquiry to the *Old Code* format, yet offer more elegance and a natural style of conversation, without the need for 'echo' language.

With these limiting factors in mind let us now explore some fundamental principles of *Old Code* and the expanded horizons offered by a *New Code* approach.

## English is Rubbish – beginnings of understanding from *Old Code*

English is a dreadful language – in fact all languages are rubbish!

Verbal communication washes over people like a wave of noise. Listeners get the broad idea of meaning from a communicator, and rarely the detail. Detail of meaning is often hidden or omitted and so messages in conversation or writing become generalised.

Spoken words can be ambiguous, uncertain, non-specific and generalised in meaning. Because our language system is so full of ambiguity and generalisation, it is easy for our transmitted communication to be misinterpreted by a person or persons with whom we are communicating. That's to say, interpreted by the message receiver in a way the transmitter did not intend. When we become the recipient of someone else's communication, we can experience the full effect of ambiguity and generalisation.

How many times have you heard someone say: 'I didn't mean it like that!' Often the language used in a conversation is so ambiguous or generic we have to ask questions to gain a more precise understanding of meaning. Even after asking a clarification question, we may find we have to ask additional, probing questions to gain what we believe to be an adequate amount of precision in our understanding. It can be hard work!

If, for example, we were to ask a colleague about their journey into work today, they may say: 'It was ok, not too bad'. What does that mean, specifically? We have received a broad generalised message telling us very little about our colleague's experience. If we asked more specific questions we'd receive more precise information back, perhaps describing the nature of the colleague's journey, the flow of traffic, road conditions, weather, temporary traffic lights and so on.

In Continue & Begin Fast Coaching we use the words 'specifically', 'precisely' and 'exactly' to encourage our coachee to be specific, precise and exact in describing an idea with precision.

*Specific* questions provide *specific* answers and creates *specific* outcomes for our *specific* coachee.

## Fuzzy Language – Building on *Old Code*

FUZZY LANGUAGE

When it comes to accuracy of meaning, the English language is often an imprecise and blunt instrument.

Most linguists will agree that English is a flexible language, in that it can be adapted to describe ideas through the use of complex sentence construction. True. However, English – like many language systems – has limited individual words to describe ideas. As a result of the limitations of language, we often find that a word or phrase can be interpreted in different ways. In the process of communicating accurately it is important that we have precision.

In Continue & Begin Fast Coaching it is vital we gain, as accurately as possible, a close approximation of the coachee's meaning. The imperfections of the English language make this challenging for the coach. Coachees, just like everyone else, use what is called 'fuzzy language'; that is, language that can have two or even multiple meanings.

Take a look at the statements below:

- I'm just not that confident.
- I'm good at preparation.
- I'm not sure what to do about it.
- It's what to say that I struggle with.
- I'm ok with people I know.
- It's the process that's so difficult to remember.
- I need to be better at using the software.

Remember, each coachee has a vivid hallucination of what she is dreaming. Each descriptive word is entirely valid in the mind of the coachee (and perhaps you, the reader) and yet there is a vagueness about the words that allows ambiguity and difference in meaning to exist, and leads to that most dangerous of coaching strategies – assuming you know what the coachee means. Is your hallucination of meaning the same as that of your coachee?

What precisely do these phrases mean? Continue & Begin Fast Coaching professionals will recognise these descriptions as being fuzzy and will make a mental note to ask good questions to gain greater precision of understanding and a more accurate reflection of the coachee's hallucination.

Using the word 'specifically' is a good starting point.

**Q.** When you say 'it's the process that's so difficult to remember', what do you have in mind, specifically?

Continue & Begin Fast Coaching professionals use fuzzy-language-busting questions to gain clarity and a better understanding of the customer's hallucination. In *New Code* there is greater emphasis on this activity.

Let's explore fuzzy language in more detail.

# *New Code* awareness – *Deletion*

When we communicate, we inadvertently (and sometimes intentionally) deliver an impoverished version of meaning. We minimise opportunities for understanding through our poor accuracy of language. This is a common feature of coachee communication. Coachees do this through precision failures, one of which may be defined as *deletion*.

*Deletion* is an omission of parts of an intended message. The speaker does not include important information in the transmission. Here are some examples, with the final example followed by a useful Deletion Buster question:

- I need some help.
- If I could just get better at it.
- I don't know what to do.
- It's never going to work.

- It's too difficult.
- Today was awful.
- I just don't feel up to it.
- They know I don't like it.
- The project isn't going well.

> **Q.** Which project isn't going well? In what way, specifically, is it not going well? What causes you to think it's not going well?

Notice how these spoken statements are missing important additional content – the *deletion* of the full representation of meaning.

Coachees are no different from any other group of people; we all delete from time to time. In fact, it's a wonder we manage to communicate effectively at all!

Impoverished communication occurs in all forms of human interaction, but when it impacts on personal performance it's time to take action to improve understanding and take targeted action.

## Seeking precision – asking *specificity questions*

If you've built up rapport and trust, your coachee is more likely to reveal her inner thinking. Asking good questions helps to uncover the experience, meaning or feeling of your coachee.

Few coaches have been trained to address *deletion* language. Fortunately it's a relatively simple skill set to learn. Let's take some impoverished statements listed in the *deletion* examples above and add in a few more. Getting inside your coachee's world can be helped by using *specificity questions*.

The *specificity questions* proposed below will provide more information to work with, offering a greater chance of exploring choices and options. Notice the use of the words *how, what, which, specifically, exactly, precisely.* Remember, we're not solution-finding at this stage, simply gaining clarity of meaning from the coachee.

> I need some help on this.
> **Q.** Ok, you need help regarding **what, specifically**?

If I could just get better at it.

**Q. What specifically** would you like to be better at? In **what** way **precisely**?

I don't know what to do.

**Q.** You don't know what to do about **what, specifically**?

It's never going to work.

**Q.** In what **way** is it not going to work, **exactly**?

It's too difficult.

**Q.** In **what** way is it too difficult?

Today was awful.

**Q. How** was it awful, **exactly**?

I just don't feel up to it.

**Q. What precisely** do you not feel up to?

They know I don't like it.

**Q. Who specifically**? **What** is it you think they know you don't like, **exactly**? **How** do you know that they know you don't like it?

I need some help.

**Q.** Ok, great, **how** can I help you **exactly**?

I'm struggling with the kids.

**Q.** Ok, **what specifically** about the kids are you struggling with?

It's no good, I can't do it.

**Q. What** is it you say you can't do, **exactly**?

My health is suffering because of this.

**Q.** In **what** way **exactly** is your health suffering? **What specifically** is it that is causing your health to suffer?

I don't have enough confidence to make presentations.

**Q.** Confidence to make **which** sort of presentations, **exactly**?

I can't close; I'm just rubbish at asking for the business.

**Q.** In **which** circumstances, **specifically**, do you think you are rubbish at asking for the business?

I need to get this finalised soon; it's urgent.

**Q.** Ok, **when specifically** would you like it finalised by?

I'm not clever enough to go to university.

**Q.** Not clever enough to do **what** at university, **exactly**?

## Transformational Grammar – Basic Application in *New Code*

*Deletion* was highlighted in a linguistic science known as *Transformational Grammar*, pioneered by Noam Chomsky in the 1950s. Transformational Grammar is a sector of linguistics that interrogates the *surface structure* of (particularly spoken) language. For our purposes we need concern ourselves only with simple elements of transformational grammar.

Chomsky (and subsequently others) identified *deletion* in everyday conversational speech as a limiting factor in effective, precise communication. It's a *pattern which connects* with helping people to develop through coaching.

In addition to *deletion*, transformational grammar identified other limiting factors including *generalisation* and *distortion*. These ideas were crystallised in Richard Bandler and John Grinder's early work in NLP.

## Generalisations

*Generalisations* include sweeping statements, statements that minimise detail, which make collective sets or offer non-specific commentary.

Here are some examples, with the final example followed by a useful Generalisation Buster question:

- People take advantage of me.
- Senior managers don't know what they're talking about.
- He always does it.

Statements that include 'universal quantifiers', such as; never, always, no one, nobody, everyone, everybody, all, none, e.g.

- She never shows up on time.
- You always say that.
- It's happened every time.

Nobody listens to what I say.

**Q.** Which people don't listen to what you say? Who specifically? What you say about what? What causes you to say people don't listen to you?

## Distortions

*Distortions* include assumptions we make about people or circumstances, attempts at mind-reading, seeing things that don't exist, or choosing a selective meaning.

The following examples include a useful Distortion Buster question for the final statement:

- She ignored me this morning, she doesn't like me.
- That customer is a dreamer; I can just tell.
- The new software will mean job losses.
- I can't do it.

He didn't get his homework in on time; he doesn't care.

**Q.** How does not getting the homework in on time mean he doesn't care? When was the homework submitted? What are the reasons for the homework being submitted late?

Transformational Grammar defines a speaker's chosen words as *utterance* or *surface structure*. This language is being selected from a deeper potential set of words available to the speaker – their vocabulary relating to a given topic, or *deep structure*. *Deep structure* is formed by the speaker's available and relevant selection of words within a vocabulary to convey a meaning, feeling or intended explanation or question – their Internal Experience.

It's a bit like an iceberg: the Internal Experience stimulates a potential *deep structure* vocabulary to select from and, after searching through options, a *surface structure* utterance is selected to convey meaning. Along the way the speaker inadvertently – or perhaps purposefully – deselects other potential words and phrases from within the *deep structure*.

## Transformational Grammar

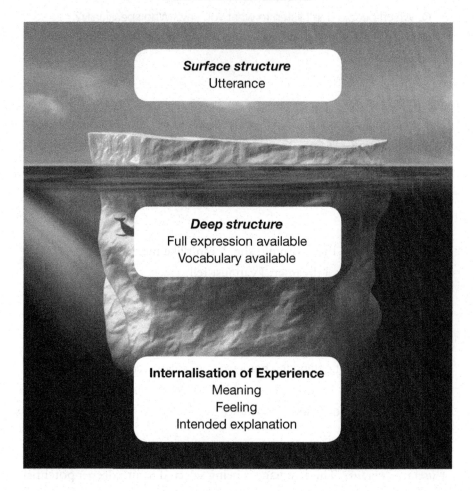

This is *deletion* in action – it's no wonder we have difficulties in understanding each other!

Most spoken human communication is pretty inaccurate. Our ability to communicate effectively is determined by our limited vocabularies and subsequent poor precision in describing meaning. Anthropologically, we've only been using vocabulary for a hundred thousand years and we're still not very good at it. Remember, we're just domesticated primates.

# Understanding Meaning
## – Seeking Precision in *New Code*

Continue & Begin Fast Coaching professionals understand the dangers of *surface structure* responses by a coachee. They ask precision questions to uncover meanings, create deeper understanding and help identify options for individuals. Continue & Begin professionals use carefully crafted language patterns to uncover a richer meaning and get as close as possible to the coachee's intended explanation – to gain greater precision of understanding.

Carl Rogers, the therapist described *understanding others* when he said,

> It means entering into the private perceptual world of the other and becoming thoroughly at home in it. It involves being sensitive, moment by moment, to the changing felt meanings which flow in this other person, to the fear or rage or tenderness or confusion or whatever that he or she is experiencing. It means temporarily living in the other's life.

To understand a coachee requires us to get inside their world. Only then will we gain a deeper understanding. Analogies in everyday language illustrate this:

- See things from their perspective.
- Look at it through their eyes.
- Think about how that sounds to them.
- Put yourself in their shoes.
- Get in touch with how they feel.
- How does this smell to them?
- Get a taste for their position on this.

Continue & Begin Fast Coaching professionals 'get inside the world' of their coachees and work hard to really understand the universe they live in.

UNDERSTAND ME...

GETTING INSIDE THE OTHER PERSON'S WORLD

- What's important to them? What's not?
- What's driving their ambitions for change? What's not?
- What do they want? What do they not want?
- What environment do they live or work in?
- What are their beliefs? Their values?
- What do they think they are doing well at? (*continue to*)
- What would they like to do differently, or improve upon? (*begin to*)

To uncover answers to these questions requires relationship dynamics of openness and trust. To achieve openness and trust in a coaching relationship it is necessary to first establish rapport.

## Rapport and Rapid Friendship – More Emphasis in *New Code*

In coaching work, practitioners have known for many years that trust and confidence between coach and coachee can only be built on the platform of an established rapport. Therapists and counsellors are trained to create rapport as the starting point for their intervention work. Clients will only open their hearts to a therapist who they feel understands, cares and empathises with them. The analogy with coaching is useful.

Rapport is a state of communication between two or more people where mutual understanding, empathy and warmth is sufficiently intense to act as a catalyst to trust. We create rapport with others when we recognise personal similarities, characteristics or lifestyle interests, which draw us together into a close neighbourhood of mutual understanding. The reality is that we like people who are like us. The idea of 'opposites attract' is rarely true in building relationships.

Rapport is a phenomenon prerequisite for successful coaching. Coachees are predisposed to 'do business' more readily with someone for whom they feel a connection than they are with someone they feel lacks understanding or empathy.

So, how can we build a relationship, even a *rapid friendship*? If we *really* listen, if we were to listen to the words, the *type* of words that people use and *how* they use them, remarkable things can happen.

## VAKOG Processing and Representation – Absent from *Old Code*

You may be familiar with visual, auditory and kinaesthetic communication styles. This idea proposes that when processing information, and at specific times, we choose a preferred 'sense' channel – either visual, auditory (hearing), kinaesthetic (feeling), olfactory (smell) or gustatory (taste) to best understand the communication message or experience.

This is one of the most commonly known propositions from NLP, co-created by Richard Bandler and John Grinder in the 1970s. NLP was originally known as META, meaning a higher, logical level of patterning – or data about data – and was concerned with the nature of communication between people and with oneself.

VAKOG is most commonly referred to as simply VAK, reflecting the widely held belief that most communication between people reflects their processing through visual, auditory and kinaesthetic representational channels.

Where VAKOG gets really interesting is the suggestion that the words we choose during conversation offer hints as to how we are processing information *at that moment in time*. This is where listening is so vital. If you listen to the words – the type of words – that people use, you can start to build a picture (visual?), to see a pattern emerging (visual?), hear a sequence (auditory?), to feel familiar feelings (kinaesthetic?) from your conversation. You can isolate word usage on the telephone quite easily.

When people describe their experiences, even in casual conversation, they are quite literal in meaning. People who say things like 'I see what you mean' are most often processing information *at that precise moment in time* in a visual mode. They have organised their internal representations in image form, and are making pictures from the words they hear.

An important note here is that representational channels in use at any given time are usually temporary and fleeting in nature. An individual is using a specific channel at that moment, in those circumstances, about that topic. These are transitory channels that may suddenly change. Please do not fall into the trap that some education providers have done of labelling a person as a 'visual learner', or having an 'auditory preference', a 'kinaesthetic thinker' or similar. British schools have made enormous errors of judgement in applying a misinterpreted version of VAK in misguided attempts to help students. A child is not a 'kinaesthetic learner' any more than she is an auditory or visual or olfactory or gustatory learner. Representational preferences are temporarily adjusted to fit an environment, that's all. Rant over.

It is amazing what we can learn about other people's communication patterns. If you haven't done so already, choose someone on whom to test this out. Become conscious of their clue words *at that specific time* and *in that specific environment,* and identify their most highly valued or dominant communication style in that moment. You can now have tremendous fun matching your representation system with theirs.

Most people, when they first do this successfully, get a real buzz of excitement in matching systems. You will quickly discover how easy it is to build a rapport with your 'experiments'. It's great fun and it builds relationships and trust. You will need to practise it to master it completely, so why not start today? Identify the representation system (at that given moment) of the next person you meet.

Here's a list of what are known as *predicate* words: I prefer to call them 'clue' words.

- **Visual Clues**
  See, look(s), sight, appears, show, reveals, make out, glimpse, recognise, shiny, dull, dark, bright, illuminates, illustrates, clear, sparkly, flash, observe, study, examine, face, overlook, peep, view.

- **Auditory Clues**
  Listen, hear, sounds, speak, talk, conversation, chat, inform, tell, deaf, quiet, noisy, lend, question, overtone, rumour, gossip, attentive.

- **Kinaesthetic Clues**
  Feel, touch, caress, finger, fondle, handle, manipulate, grasp, grip, hold, slip, catch, tap, contact, throw, harsh, soft, tough, thick, thin, fancy, empathy, sympathy, catch.

Here are some phrases you can interpret on your own.

- How do you feel about this?
- In my mind's eye.
- This sounds strange.
- Get an eyeful of this.
- In a manner of speaking.
- What does that say to you?

- Can you get to grips with this?
- I don't follow you.
- Looks about right.
- Feels Ok to me.
- I see what you're saying.
- How does that sound to you?
- He's a pain in the neck.
- That's rather short sighted of him.
- I don't see how it could.
- Catch a glimpse of this.
- Give me an account of it.
- That's how it looks to me.
- There's a hidden message here.

How about this though: one of my friends has a habit of referring to how a situation *tastes* to him. What representational system is he using at that moment in time? How could you respond in a similar style?

We sometimes talk about being 'in sync' with someone. You probably remember times when you knew exactly what someone was thinking or what they were about to say. Perhaps you even went to say the same words as them. Chances are you were using the same representational system at that moment, and were in deep rapport.

Establish the communication system someone is using and then adapt yours to suit. It seems so simple, yet it requires concentration and practice until it becomes second nature; until you become unconsciously competent.

## 'Clean' Language – A Simplified Approach

VAK patterning can be hard work when you first start out. Representational systems have a habit of shifting about during conversation and it takes concentrated effort (initially) to recognise a person's current communication channel and to respond appropriately in a timely manner. A much easier strategy for building rapport is to use *clean language*.

**CLEAN LANGUAGE**

*Clean language* is a rapport-building technique employing a simple principle: if I use the same words as you, *particularly when you use idioms, analogies or metaphors,* then we have a greater possibility of creating a rapid rapport, based on mutual use of language.

The less we try to paraphrase or adapt the language used by other people into our own preferred language, and the more we use their chosen words and sentence construction, the more likely it is that our fellow communicators will feel a sense of understanding and empathy from us.

This has proven to be a powerful rapport-building technique. Where possible, key words from the speaker's language patterns are repeated back by the rapport builder. The skill is in identifying which words to repeat back and when, in order for the other person to feel that the process is a natural activity rather than a conscious and contrived technique.

At any time during a conversation you have the opportunity to 'use the words the speaker uses' in order to confirm and demonstrate that you do understand what she is saying.

**Customer**: Hello, it's that time of year again I'm afraid. *Every year* it's a worry. I wonder how *expensive* it's going to be for servicing. I always think it will *cost the earth*.

Service adviser: Ok, let's see if I can help you. There's no need for it to *cost the earth*. Our fixed-price servicing plan is a great way to budget so it doesn't have to be *expensive every year.* You know exactly how much it's going to cost, and it will take the worry away for you.

Get the idea? *Clean language* is hugely powerful if delivered in a natural style. We know that we can quietly echo some key words, often mid-way through a speaker's delivery, perhaps with a nodding head that gives the impression of true, empathetic understanding. Using the other person's idioms, analogies, metaphors and colloquialisms is a great way to build a relationship.

We can also ask questions of co-communicators, using their already-spoken words and phrases, to clarify our understanding of their thoughts and at the same time confirming to her we have listened – after all, we must have listened, because we are using their words!

*Clean language* emphasises to the other person that we have listened and that we 'speak the same language'. It's a great rapport-building technique.

## Confidence and Motivation

People with low self-image tend to have low motivation. Fact.

When I was facilitating tutorials with management students, the more they spoke about the burdens they were carrying, the pressure of work, their employers' emphasis on continuous improvement in everything they did and the stress levels they were experiencing, so their physiology and posture changed downwards, their breathing reduced in frequency and volume and their language became focused on negativity. They were concerned about *failure*.

For some, their employer's expectations evolved into (perceived) threatening demands, followed by layer upon layer of additional tasks. This is not a fertile environment in which to explore personal development and growth.

Asking people with low belief about *self* to take on significant personal change is a recipe for disaster. This is why Continue & Begin Fast Coaching is structured the way it is. We start with mandatory celebration – an emphasis on identifying and enjoying examples of recent personal success, no matter how trivial.

We build up *continue to* successes until the coachee's ego is strong and the physiology, posture, breathing patterns and language have changed to those of personal empowerment. It is critical to the success of the *begin to* stage that the ego is strong enough to take on new ambitions. Without this in place the coachee is hamstrung by self-doubt and scepticism about the realism of new ambitions.

## The Emotional Driver in Continue & Begin Fast Coaching

EMOTIONAL DRIVER

It is a truism that all human behaviour has a positive intent – that is, people do things for a reason. The reason is not always obvious to the outsider and sometimes is not even consciously recognised by the person exhibiting the behaviour.

Behaviour is driven by an underlying emotional need – an Emotional Driver – encouraging us to make a movement towards emotional pleasure, or a movement away from existing or anticipated psychological pain.

Although we are not always consciously aware, there is also a physical feeling associated with emotional comfort or discomfort. Scientists have proven that the feel-good factor quickly translates into physical well-being. By contrast, when we feel down, we sometimes experience symptoms of physical illness.

Emotion influences human behaviour. Our emotions and the physical feelings they evoke can be highly influential in our behavioural decisions. Behaviour is driven by our emotions.

A key skill for Continue & Begin Fast Coaching professionals is to understand the thoughts and feelings a coachee has as they consider making a commitment to take action. Coachees will commit to a personal-change plan if the emotional pay-off is sufficient to stimulate and sustain new action; they will if there is a strong enough Emotional Driver. What is an Emotional Driver?

## Moving Away and Moving Towards

Every coachee's decision to take action is based on one of two internal motivators, what I call Emotional Drivers – either:

- Movement away from pain or discomfort – including fear of potential future pain or discomfort; or
- Movement towards pleasure – as feelings of relaxation, comfort or contentment.

### Movement away from pain

This is a coachee's planned movement away from anxiety, from discomfort, or from physical or emotional pain. It may be driven by a fear of future

MOVEMENT AWAY FROM DISCOMFORT/PAIN

anxiety, discomfort and physical or emotional pain. This is almost always an unconscious processing activity going on.

We know emotional or psychological pain is experienced physiologically. When we are under stress our bodies react to protect us. We prepare at an unconscious level for the potential need to fight or run away when faced with danger – the classic fight or flight response.

We react to our physiological, security and social needs in a manner that we (unconsciously) believe will remove or minimise unwelcome feelings. We respond as any sensible mammal would do – to move away from pain. Robert Anton Wilson was right when he described humans as domesticated primates (*Prometheus Rising*, 1983). This applies absolutely to coachees.

Incidentally, there is a third response, specifically related to fear of future pain, which is *play dead*. Few people are consciously aware of this response mechanism and yet it is prevalent in our everyday living when, in a socially or professionally threatening environment, we exhibit:

- minimised movement
- low-level breathing (minimal chest movement)
- avoidance of eye contact.

61

These are all physiological strategies to avoid being seen or heard: to play dead. It happens at work all the time; the employee whose self-talk goes:

> Oh! She's in a mood, I'd better keep my head down … I'll be 'low profile' busy … tap, tap gently on the keyboard … avoid eye contact … don't move too much … don't breathe too much … don't want to be significant at this moment.

## Movement towards pleasure

MOVEMENT TOWARDS COMFORT/PLEASURE

Some coachees will have a specific 'pleasure feeling' they wish to access. Maybe it's a feeling of achievement, of pleasure associated with recognition for achievement, of status, of security, of ego, of contentment, or maybe exhilaration or excitement.

What is the best, most accurate description (using the coachee's language) of the pleasure that will stimulate their movement towards new behaviour?

# The Emotional Driver for Your Coachee?

Movement away? Movement towards? Which is it?

Sometimes it's both, but one is always the dominant force. Think about it; consider every piece of behaviour you are exhibiting now – every single movement or action is in furtherance of one or both of these two mammalian drivers. Let's illustrate this:

| Behaviour/Activity | Movement away or movement towards | Purpose |
|---|---|---|
| Shift position in chair | Movement away | Remove pressure on thigh or buttock |
| | Movement towards | Feel blood return to thigh or buttock |
| Make a cup of tea | Movement away | Remove discomfort of dry throat |
| | Movement towards | Enjoy pleasure of tea taste |
| **In education** Complete next homework assignment in required format, to required standard, submitted on time | Movement towards | Feelings of achievement, satisfaction, ego, self-worth, self-image, contentment |
| | Movement away | Remove anxiety, fear of poor academic results |
| **In family life** Provide children with breakfast and clean school uniform each morning this week | Movement towards | Feel good about being a caring parent, pride in family performance, enjoy time with family, knowing you're doing your best for your children |
| | Movement away | Remove feelings of parental low esteem, self-image and self-worth |

| Behaviour/Activity | Movement away or movement towards | Purpose |
| --- | --- | --- |
| **In health and well-being** Cycle 10 miles twice a week during next month | Movement away | Remove work-related stress feeling |
| | Movement towards | Enjoy pleasure of outdoors, breathing easier, pride |
| **In business** Ask 'qualification' questions of all prospective customers | Movement towards | Confidence in professionalism, fulfil ambition of achieving sales targets, feel achievement, feel secure in role |
| | Movement away | Remove discomfort associated with recent/future poor sales performance, reduced anxiety related to insecurity of income |

Is the coachee driven by an urge to move away from discomfort? Or is she planning some pleasure? What is the Emotional Driver for taking action in her Continue & Begin personal development?

Remember – coachees commit to take action for one or both of these reasons. What's driving the potential change behaviour of your coachee? What's the dominant force? Movement away from discomfort or movement towards pleasure?

## Analogue Marking to Enhance Communication

Milton Erickson is known as the father of modern hypnotherapy and was the master of analogue marking. He is the creator of what is sometimes called conversational hypnosis.

Erickson used non-verbal cues to complement his verbal and tonal emphasis. By subtle shifts in body position, direction of speech and using minor motor movements, he would covertly 'mark' significant messages in his communication to create emphasis. The mark would be recognised unconsciously by his patient – not at a conscious level of thought. Erickson was a sophisticated communicator and catalyst of personal change.

In *New Code* Continue & Begin Fast Coaching we use analogue marking as an *overt* non-verbal message in three simple patterns. I use these patterns intuitively in *Old Code*; in *New Code* we promote the patterns explicitly to each new Certified Coach.

## Analogue mark – pattern 1

At the start of self-assessment a coachee will sometimes (often!) respond by highlighting her development needs – a stimulus response to being asked about her performance. A skilled Continue & Begin coach will take hold of an imaginary 'box' of the coachee's development needs and move them to one side, accompanied by the instruction:

> Let's park these over here for now. We can review those later. Now, what were you pleased with?

## Analogue mark – pattern 2

At *begin to* time, we can return to the 'box of development needs'. We can take hold of the box (remember, placed to one side earlier) and bring it back to centre stage:

> Now, there were a few things you wanted to think about doing differently ...

## Analogue mark – pattern 3

We use a hand movement to initiate thinking about something new. By making a circling motion of the hand, palm down, we can talk about:

> There may be some things you'd like to [or, You said you wanted to ...] do differently ... and [raising the arm upwards pointing towards a higher plane] maybe even better.

The analogue mark focuses attention and stimulates thinking about performance improvement.

## Analogue mark – pattern 4

During Can't to Can Belief Busting we can use an analogue mark to initiate an exploration of possibility. This is a key stage in Can't to Can and a mark can work wonders in stimulating thoughts of future potential.

At the benefits stage of Can't to Can (in *New Code* see *future feeling*) we can ease the coachee's passage towards accepting *at least the possibility* of 'Can' by asking her to:

> ... just imagine for a moment, some future time and place where you
> can do that thing ... [skill, activity, competency, behaviour] ...

As we ask the question we can look up, raising our arm – palm upwards – and stare far into the distance with an expression of awe and wonderment. The impact of this little piece of drama is an increased likelihood that the coachee will accept there may be a future time and space where it is *at least possible* to do 'the thing' she has initially said she *can't do*.

## Analogue mark – pattern 5

At *future feeling* stage in both Continue & Begin and Can't to Can we can use a simple analogue mark to emphasise feeling by leaning forward and holding our hand to our heart as we ask the question:

> And how will that make you feel, being able to do that really well?

The verbal question is reinforced by the non-verbal mark.

## Analogue mark – pattern 6

At action plan stage in both Continue & Begin and Can't to Can it is essential we gain a definitive commitment to do the thing she said she would do. Our analogue mark here is a simple one, it is to lock on with laser vision and look deeply into the coachee's eyes as we ask whichever commitment question the coach thinks appropriate for the circumstances and the coachee, for example,

Is this something you're going to do?

This is a super-assertive mark which leaves the coachee in no doubt the coach is serious about implementation as well as verbal commitment. Immediately after the intense eye contact we can alleviate any discomfort by smiling and making a light hearted comment such as:

Well that's good, alright then!

or similar.

Analogue marks are powerful non-verbal communication patterns, which impact at an unconscious level. Used well they add panache and elegance to the Continue & Begin coach's communication repertoire.

## *Yes Sets* and the Regulation of Thinking

Building self-worth and self-image is a core ambition of Continue & Begin Fast Coaching. When a person feels good about herself ambition for further personal development becomes less daunting, even appealing! Virginia Satir, the celebrated family therapist, observed similarly:

I am convinced that the crucial factor in what happens both inside people and between people is the picture of individual worth that each person carries around with him ...
*Peoplemaking*, Satir, V., Science and Behaviour Books, 1972

The language pattern 'And what else?' in Continue & Begin Fast Coaching is an example of building a pattern of affirmations to build recognition of successes and create a resultant enhanced perception of self. The pattern may be presented in a variety of guises:

- Tell me some more things that went well.
- Think about [explicit operating standards, agreed goals, stated ambitions]. Which were you able to implement, fully or partially?
- What about X? [when evidence suggests success] How did that go?
- I bet there were other things you were pleased with. What were they?

It is this building of patterns of success that develops a momentum of productive thinking and a gradual layering of positive well-being. The process becomes easier as it progresses to mirror a *yes set* of regulated thinking – a habit of thinking positively about self, an attitude of repeated recognition of personal achievement, no matter how small.

Dmitri (Dmitry Nikolaevich) Uznadze was a Georgian psychologist (1886–1950). In his research paper *Theory of Attitude and Set* Uznadze illustrated how repetitive mental habit creates an embedded pattern of thinking. During a series of experiments he had students handle a pair of balls placed simultaneously in his or her hand and say which was the larger.

> The balls are presented several (ten to fifteen) times so that the set or disposition (to identify the big one and the small one) induced on each occasion becomes sufficiently well reinforced (these are set-inducing tests), after which 'say the sixteenth time', the original balls of different sizes are replaced by two of identical size, although the subject is still asked to compare their sizes.
>
> This test usually reveals that the subject has acquired a fixed set corresponding to the previous tests and now judges one of the two equal-sized balls to be 'larger' or 'smaller'. The set-inducing tests have created a state producing the illusionary perception that equal-sized balls are of different sizes.
>
> PROSPECTS: *The Quarterly Review of Comparative Education* (Paris, UNESCO: International Bureau of Education), vol. 24, no.3/4, 1994, p. 687–701 UNESCO: International Bureau of Education, 2002

In Continue & Begin Fast Coaching we use *yes set* thinking to build up a pattern of positivity for our coachee. You may be curious, 'What else?' could you use *yes set* thinking for?

# *Nudging* – Greater Emphasis in *New Code*

*Old Code* Continue & Begin referred in passing to *nudging.* In *New Code* greater emphasis is given to this activity.

Continue & Begin Fast Coaching creates confidence and motivation through inner recognition of achievement and the celebration of success. We encourage the coachee to wallow unashamedly in feel-good and enhanced ego before considering how their future personal performance could become even better through a small number of *begin to* changes of behaviour.

Instrumental in this process is the identification of a series of *continue to* behaviours in which the coachee has already proven competence. If someone can do something once, they can do it again. They already have the internal technology and personal strategies to repeat their excellence.

The challenge, for some coachees, is reluctance to allow themselves the temerity of self-congratulation. Many individuals have internal software programmes, honed over decades, which prevent personal applause and congratulation. There is a self-imposed resistance to personal praise, born of a fear of appearing arrogant. In many societies self-deprecation has its own charm and value – except when it gets in the way of self-image and self-worth.

In Continue & Begin Fast Coaching we seek out evidence of personal success and build up a *yes set* of achievements to help the coachee acknowledge their existing, perhaps previously unrecognised, patterns of success.

When a coachee gets stuck, and 'Can't think of anything else', that's where a well-timed *nudge* will move her towards evidence of competence – evidence already identified by the fast coach. *Nudging* can take a number of forms, including language patterns that focus attention on known competences. Experienced Continue & Begin fast coaches will use analogue marking and non-verbal indicators as additional tools in their influencing arsenal.

Typical verbal *nudges* are:

- How did you get on with ...?
- Presenting is an important part of what you do. How did that go?
- I noticed you ...
- What were the marking criteria for that assignment?
- Tell me about ...
- What does our customer service charter say?
- I noticed you were reading a story to Aimee ...
- What are the Family Ambitions on cooking/washing up/cleaning?
- Tell me, what was happening there?
- Think back to your induction training course ... what were you able to implement?
- What is our process for that situation?
- How are you getting on with ...?
- One of the things you said/did was ...
- Tell me about X.

When it comes to *begin to* behaviours, *nudging* is equally valuable in helping the coachee self-identify key and significant opportunities to develop; specifically *significant* development opportunities, not just a trivial change. We only have a few *begin to* opportunities to work with, so let's make sure they are worthwhile activities. We may need to *nudge* the coachee towards them.

*Nudging* is a very cool tool!

# Can't to Can Belief Busting
# and Modal Operators of Possibility

Questions within the Can't to Can Belief Busting model are carefully crafted to stimulate changes in thinking. I often refer to two specific Can't to Can questions as *freedom questions* as they encourage the coachee to think about possibility and opportunity. These questions are:

● 'What would happen if you could?' This is a stimulus to think about a future state where a new reality exists.
● 'What would have to happen to make that happen?' This is a stimulus to think about strategy to achieve a desired future state.

These questions originate from transformational grammar. The TG description for these types of questions is Modal Operators of Possibility. Examples of Modal Operators of Possibility include:

● What if you did?
● What if you could?
● What would happen if you …?
● What would have to happen for you to …?

There is a flipside to Modal Operators of Possibility, known as Modal Operators of Necessity. These are the statements made by people who have impoverished maps of their territory. Modal Operators of Necessity statements might include:

● I can't …
● I mustn't …
● I shouldn't …
● I have to …

Where we hear a statement that is a Modal Operator of Necessity we can use Modal Operators of Possibility to unblock the limited thinking:

- What would happen if you didn't? [... comply with that restriction]
- What would happen if you did? [... do that thing]

Modal Operators are a great way to unlock potential. That's why Can't to Can Belief Busting is so powerful.

## 'I Know You Don't Know ...' – A Special Tool for Unblocking Thought

A pattern that connects Can't to Can and Continue & Begin core questions is the tendency of individuals to respond to coaching questions with a classic linguistic forward defensive of 'I don't know'. This manifests itself in communication like this:

> What are you pleased with?
> Dunno

Or,

> What would have to happen to make that happen?
> Dunno

This initial response is often a habit-ual thinking pattern. As the Continue & Begin practitioner encourages the coachee to build up a *yes set* of *continue to*'s or sets out to get things moving in Can't to Can, a coachee may offer a negative response as her default setting.

This limitation creates a habit pattern. It's a pattern that presents itself in restrictions of possibility. It's easier for the individual to accept her status quo – after all, she is familiar with it! A person may wish for change, to have some altered reality, and yet for many people their desire to have something greatly exceeds their desire to do something about it.

When you're confronted with a 'dunno responder' a helpful language pattern to unlock potential is to acknowledge the initial 'dunno' response and then ask the person to imagine or pretend a more resourceful state in which to operate. By accessing the 'pretend' resourceful state, coachees discover a parallel world of possibility.

'I know you don't know ... but [inverse use of But Monster] if you did know ... what would you say [you are pleased with/would have to happen]?'

'I know you don't know/if you did know' is safe and unthreatening because it's not asking for real action, just an imaginary resourceful state where positivity becomes more accessible.

So, as a Continue & Begin fast coach, how are you going to use this new language pattern? What's that you say? You don't know? Ok, well I know you don't know ... but if you did know ... how would you say you could use it?

## Diversity of Application – Example Action Plans

Continue & Begin started life as a personal-change tool for mature students before moving on to applications for business managers in the former Soviet Union, then small business entrepreneurs in the UK and subsequently commercial applications, including business-to-consumer (B2C) environments involving customer service and retail sales operations. My book *Boomerang!* described in some detail how Continue & Begin Fast Coaching is effectively applied in these contexts.

*New Code* emphasises the opportunity to use Continue & Begin in a much wider set of contexts than previously recognised. Appendix 1 to this book provides an overview of typical applications of *New Code* Continue & Begin in a range of environments, with example action plans from sectors including families, healthcare, leisure, school, sport and housing environments, as well as customer service and sales.

As a taster, described below is an example of an action plan created by Liesel, a high-achieving Year 11 (age 15) high school student in the UK. Liesel has created an action plan as an output from being fast-coached by a school teaching support worker trained in the use of Continue & Begin Fast Coaching. Liesel's plan centres on preparations for her year 11 exams.

**School (Academic Year 11)**

| Continue & Begin Fast Coaching Action Plan | |
|---|---|
| **Liesel** | **Year 11 exam prep** |
| *continue to* | Keep up attendance above 95% |
| *continue to* | Arrive at school before 8.30 |
| *continue to* | Submit Y11 coursework on time |
| *continue to* | Practise French with Sarah at dancing |
| *continue to* | Read English Lit every Sun from now till Easter |
| *continue to* | Help with choreography at Rock Challenge |
| **Celebrate this!** | |
| begin to 1 | Use Outlook diary for scheduling revision |
| What has to happen? | Have a practice session this Saturday 10am |
| begin to 2 | Do 1 old exam paper each week until mocks |
| What has to happen? | Diarise which subject papers when |
| begin to 3 | Finish coursework 1 week b4 deadlines |
| What has to happen? | Set up Outlook timetable |
| *Commitment is doing the thing you said you would do, long after the mood you said it in has left you!* | |
| Review date: | |

# PART 2

## how to use
## *fast coaching*

# *New Code* Continue & Begin Fast Coaching Learning Content

Part 2 of this book offers a summary of key learning points contained within a *New Code* training event or conference presentation. This is reverse engineering: it's an online-learning training programme transcribed into a book!

The learning content here comes from a series of face-to-camera video presentations I gave to help new users understand the basic principles and activities required to deliver an outstanding *New Code* Continue & Begin Fast Coaching session. The presentations were made as follow-up material for learners using a *New Code* workbook; these workbooks are mentioned throughout this section but reference to them should be ignored. As these verbal presentations have been transcribed into text, punctuation and grammar is conversational and is best read with my spoken voice in mind.

Presentation to camera isn't always the best way to transfer technology, so in a few instances, where it makes sense to do so, I've provided narrative from a recorded (live) Continue & Begin training event. As described above, the text is conversational in format and style.

## Context Awareness

Before we get into the presentations, let's quickly review the typical contexts within which Continue & Begin Fast Coaching can be effectively deployed. Continue & Begin is a *content-free* model and so the methodologies described may be applied with equal effect in a diverse range of circumstances, as demonstrated in the examples that follow.

### At work
These include commercial, public sector or third (voluntary) sector business environments, including B2C and Business-to-Business (B2B) contexts. World-class brands already embrace Continue & Begin Fast Coaching as their preferred methodology for developing people and creating sustainability of

outstanding performance, which is so important to business. Continue & Begin is so popular in the workplace because of its speed of application, the feel-good sense of well-being it evokes and the business imperatives on which it delivers.

## In the family

Continue & Begin is used extensively in family coaching and group therapies, where brief intervention is the ideal. Intermediary groups providing support to families – including those engaged with criminal justice agencies or on the brink of criminality – provide self-worth coaching and aspirational encouragement through the use of Continue & Begin. In 'ordinary' families, advocates describe the 'blossoming' of children and adults as they celebrate their successes – no matter how small they may seem to outsiders – and build up a sense of achievement and resultant self-worth. When family members feel good about themselves and their siblings, parents and children, amazing, positive things can happen!

## In the community

Community, housing and care agencies recognise the opportunities Continue & Begin provides in helping tenants and service-users to take responsibility for their own lifestyle, behaviour choices and the nature of their living accommodation. By developing (often long-suppressed) ego through identification of *continue to* behaviours, even the most self-critical individuals can begin the process of building self-worth and self-image.

## In health and well-being

Continue & Begin is now used as a well-being catalyst, helping users of healthcare services to celebrate their accomplishments and move towards more fulfilling lives, taking more personal ownership for their health and happiness. Cumulatively this has a beneficial effect on healthcare service provision, reducing resource requirements in key areas of public health need.

## In education

The education setting is the most untapped of all opportunities. When schools, colleges and other educational establishments take on a co-ordinated (as opposed to ad hoc) approach to embracing Continue & Begin principles, we will see phenomenal improvements in children's and young persons' psychological well-being and attitude to personal development, way beyond a purely academic impact. This is such an enormous opportunity that it consumes me with hope and frustration in equal measure.

So, with the above in mind, enjoy the following guided learning transcripts from a series of video presentations. The transcripts are copied verbatim from the film clips, so expect 'spoken' English, with all its colloquialisms, mannerisms and shortcuts on grammar you would hear when someone speaks rather than writes.

As the hypnotherapist Milton Erickson would say, 'My voice will go with you'. If it is helpful you may wish to 'prime' your mind by listening to my voice via www.continueandbegin.com or check out my channel on YouTube.

Enjoy the learning!

# Guided Learning Video Presentation Transcripts

## Welcome to *New Code* Continue & Begin Fast Coaching

Hello everyone, I'm Nick. Welcome to Continue & Begin Fast Coaching!

I'm delighted you're here to join us and learn the Continue & Begin Fast Coaching method. I know you're going to really enjoy this learning and you'll be able use it in your role as a fast coach to benefit others. It's a wonderful gift.

What you're about to learn can make phenomenal differences to the way people lead their lives ... in more productive, happier and more fulfilling ways than they thought possible.

First up, let me share a little bit of history with you ... When I was a lecturer back in the 90s I had no idea I was creating a fast coaching method for my students that would go on to benefit so many people, in such diverse environments. My book *Boomerang!* published back in 2007, explained Continue & Begin using customer service as an illustration.

Of course, Continue & Begin is used in wider contexts – social care, housing, in education and sport, and in families. Continue & Begin Fast Coaching continually develops as a feel-good fast coaching method. It's important (you know this) to grow and improve.

*Old Code* Continue & Begin has done a fine job and it's now time to move over and make way for *New Code* Continue & Begin Fast Coaching. *New Code* includes insights from my personal delivery patterns. My patterns evolved from decades of studying the masters of personal change – people like Frank Farrelly, Fritz Perls, Aaron Beck, Alfred Korzybski, Noam Chomsky, Virginia Satir, Milton Erickson, Richard Bandler, John Grinder and Frank Pucelik and the fabulous Tony Robbins ... and most recently the very cool people at Esalen Institute in Big Sur, California – and what a place that is!

So, *New Code* Continue & Begin goes to the next stage in effectiveness – it's an evolution. In *New Code* there's greater emphasis on 'feeling', on future orientation, and why basic strategies from *Transformational Grammar* are so helpful for Continue & Begin coaches and ultimately, of course, the people you are coaching. *Old Code* is fine ... *New Code* is where the new thinking excites everyone who's used it, and it delivers even better results!

We have a new generation of fast coaching to help people celebrate and feel good and then work towards fulfilling their dreams ... whatever the context may be.

Today there are thousands of coaches just like you, who have learned to use Continue & Begin Fast Coaching to help others grow and develop: in their work and education, in their health and well-being, their communities and in their family lives. There are some wonderful development activities going on out there, supporting people with this fabulous fast coaching method.

Why is this coaching approach so different from others? Well, Continue & Begin is simple to use, and it's fast. There are plenty of personal coaching methods, and some of them are very good. The challenge with many of them is they take time, and in today's world we have very little time. Continue & Begin Fast Coaching is quick – it takes only a few minutes to use; it's ideal for our busy lives. One organisation I know has a 4-minute rule for Continue & Begin Fast Coaching!

And as well as being time efficient, Continue & Begin has another major benefit: it makes people feel good!

When it's delivered as designed, Continue & Begin Fast Coaching builds up a person's self-image until their ego is strong and they feel confident about their skills and abilities. When someone feels good, they are much more enthusiastic about taking on next-step development. And that's what Continue & Begin does: it makes people feel good about their successes and it creates self-motivation to perform even better. And it does it quickly.

Today you'll learn how to use *New Code* Continue & Begin Fast Coaching, the very latest evolution of Continue & Begin. It's packed full of hints and tips and plenty of underpinning knowledge to help you use the method and understand why it is working.

You'll be able to start using *New Code* Continue & Begin straight away: at work, or maybe in a health or community context, in education, or perhaps helping families – even your own.

Pay attention, soak up your new knowledge and remember: knowing what to do is not the same as doing what you know. Enjoy your learning and enjoy knowing what a difference you will be making to people's lives with your new fast coaching skills.

## Channels of use

Now, there are three ways in which we can use Continue & Begin Fast Coaching – these are known as channels of use.

The first is what's called *reflective behaviour*. What does that mean? Well, it means we can use Continue & Begin Fast Coaching to help people reflect on what's been going on in their working lives or social lives or any other environment over the last few days, weeks or months. And we can use Continue & Begin to help them think about what they've been doing well and the kind of things they might want to begin to do differently, and perhaps even better. So that's the first way that we can use it: reflective behaviour.

The second way we can use Continue & Begin – the second channel – is to use it for what's called *observed behaviour* coaching. So, what does that mean? What it means is, when we see and hear somebody in action, in whatever field of endeavour they undertaking, we can then use Continue & Begin Fast Coaching, again, to help them identify what they've done well and the things they want to continue to do well, and just a couple of things they might want to do differently – perhaps even better. In some organisations Continue & Begin practitioners refer to this as in-the-moment coaching.

There's a third way that we can use Continue & Begin and that's through what's called *Recorded Practice* or *Recorded Behaviour*. It may be recorded telephone calls or maybe looking at emails or written reports – or maybe, in some circumstances, it might be video recordings.

All three of these channels use the same format, the same process, the same methodology: Continue & Begin Fast Coaching.

And as we progress through this programme you are going to learn how we can use Continue & Begin Fast Coaching in each of those three channels: reflective behaviour, observed behaviour and recorded behaviour. That's what we're going to do now.

## Contents

Ok, let's have a look in your Continue & Begin Fast Coaching workbook. What you'll see here are the contents of the programme – a great big list of things that you're going to learn today. Now there are some things in there that may seem a little strange for you, things like *chocolate praise*, like the But Monster, like the NDK Performance Model. What are these ideas?

You're going to learn all about them, and by the time we're part way through today you'll understand all of those constituent parts of the Continue & Begin approach to fast coaching.

But here's the thing: knowing what to do is not the same as doing what you know, so you'll learn the content and you'll understand it conceptually and intellectually. That's fine, but it doesn't mean you're able to use Continue & Begin Fast Coaching effectively, because what we have to do is to turn your knowledge into behaviour.

And here's the challenge. Turning knowledge into behaviour is the first part. Then what we've got to do is to make sure the new behaviour is maintained, that it is sustained, that we keep that plate spinning, we keep the momentum going. So knowing the Continue & Begin stuff is one thing, but doing it is something else – and maintaining that new doing is something else altogether. That's what we're going to do as we progress.

## The eternal training conflict

Let's take this a step further. I mentioned just now: knowing what to do is not the same as doing what you know.

The same principles about knowledge and behaviour apply to the people you will be coaching, using the Continue & Begin approach. They will have some existing knowledge about what success means for them in their world – whatever their world may be.

Chances are, they have already been taught, or trained, or in some way been introduced to a set of behaviour patterns that could reasonably be accepted as aspirational, that's to say, a way of operating that they would like to deliver on. If they haven't been introduced to these 'good practice' behaviour patterns, we may not be in a coaching situation – that's a teaching or training issue. We'll explore that dynamic in a moment.

So, if the individual has already been taught or trained, or they've been involved in the development of a set of behaviour patterns, how is it that they don't deliver on their knowledge?

You hear people all the time saying: 'Oh yeah, I went on that course'; 'Oh yeah, I remember agreeing to that'; 'Oh yeah, I read that book'; 'Oh yeah, I know that process, that activity, that way of operating'.

So why don't they do it? Well, it's because they've temporarily misfiled the knowledge or maybe they didn't file it away properly when they first learned it. Learning is only truly embedded when we apply it. That's why practice really does make perfect; you've got to do it – not just know it.

Everything we have ever experienced is already embedded on the hard drive of our minds; these embedded memories are called engrams, and they are permanently engraved traces of memory – it's just that sometimes we misfile things and they become hard to find.

Well, where has the learning gone? It's still there; it's hidden under some papers, or lost behind the radiator, or under the couch – lost somewhere in the mind.

The task of a Continue & Begin fast coach is to help a person find the lost information they already learned about. Once the coachee has the recollection we can then help her think about how she has been performing in relation to those ambitions. Continue & Begin Fast Coaching does that quickly and effectively, and leaves the coachee feeling more optimistic about what's possible.

So, the eternal training conflict, in all organisations and in domestic environments, there is a differential between what has been taught, trained and learned, and what is delivered in the form of behaviour.

Some of you will be familiar with this question from the world of work, and this continuing measurement: 'How much is the training costing and what is the return on our investment?'

*Knowing what to do is not the same as doing what you know.*

## NDK Performance Model (organisational version)

Ok, let's explore something called the NDK Performance Model.

So, here's a question for you: which organisations have a fantastic reputation for service quality – customer service quality? What kind of brands have an awesome reputation for providing world-class service experiences for their customers? Let's have a think. Companies that are often mentioned are brands like John Lewis, people like Virgin, Mercedes-Benz, Emirates Airlines – these kinds of organisations.

Now all of these brands have something in common; they have what's called a *pattern which connects*. They all have a set of explicit standards: service standards, operating standards, behaviour standards and a set of values too. Every single one of these super-brands has an expectation of their people about how employees are expected to perform. These are explicit standards.

You may have seen these described as explicit standards, service standards, promises to customers – things like that. You'll have seen them described perhaps on a wall on some form of poster, or maybe you've seen them in a glossy leaflet, something like that. But here's the thing – here's the rub of it – having the fancy stuff written down, having the explicit standards described is one thing, but unless it's turned into behaviour it's just hot air, it's just words. It means nothing. And I've worked with a lot of organisations who are not yet world class, who have got fantastic explicit standards; it's just that, frankly, those words are not turned into behaviour.

So there is the first learning point of the NDK Performance Model.

Let's get some explicit standards in place; let's help people understand how they're expected to perform. If you want to work for one of these world-class brands, make no mistake – if you want to be part of the family you will be expected to perform using those standards. You'll be expected to deliver; to behave in the way the organisation expects you to do – and those are explicit standards. So having them in place is great, but on their own they are not enough; they have to be turned into behaviour.

Now let's have a look at the second level in the NDK Performance Model.

I'm very lucky. I've got to work with different organisations all around the world, and when I meet world-class brands – and brands that aspire to become world class – I generally meet the top dog, the boss, the person responsible for service quality, and we have a conversation. It's the same conversation every time. Maybe the words change a little bit, but the essence of it is common and it goes like this. He or she will say to me:

**Boss**: Ok Nick, thanks for coming all this way. We've got a challenge.

**NDK**: Oh really, what's that?

**Boss**: Well the challenge we've got is this: you know, competition's tough; there's not a massive differential in product, or service, between us and our competitors. And the reality is that the difference that makes the difference is the calibre of our customers' experience. I've got to tell you, Nick, I've got some parts of the organisation where service quality is exemplary, it's first class, it's outstanding, they are pockets of excellence. The vast majority of my operation, though, is just ok – we're doing alright. I've got acres of mediocrity and, unfortunately, I've also got some pits of despair. No matter what I do I just can't get some people and some parts of my organisation to operate at a good level and certainly not to an excellent level. I've got inconsistency. Can you help me?

And my answer is:

Yes, of course we can help. We can help you create service delivery at a very high level indeed – which is consistent. We can do that by high-impact, fantastic, different training – the kind of training that most people have not experienced before. But here's the thing: the training, the impact of training, is temporary; it doesn't last long.

Now … hah! The truth is, this training is a waste of time, did you know that? Particularly soft skills training and customer service training – a complete waste of time. It's like throwing wet mud up against the wall: most of it slides off immediately. It leaves a bit of sediment behind, and there's a big puddle of brown water on the floor. Training doesn't work.

Now if you're from L&D or HR – you know, human remains – you may be feeling a little bit uncomfortable at the moment, but bear with me.

It's true! When people leave a training environment – as they walk out the door – I see it so regularly: the learning is falling off them even as they exit the room. It doesn't stick. Training doesn't work.

It's ok L&D and HR people, there's an upside – they're all sat there thinking: 'What? You mean there's hope?' Ha ha! Yes, there is.

Because, here's the thing: when L&D – when training – is turned into behaviour, and then the behaviour is sustained, now … *now* the training becomes valuable; *now* it's gold; *now* you get a return on investment the like of which you've never had before. But it has to be sustained, and that's the final part – the top of the pyramid of the NDK Performance Model – where we create sustainability. That's essentially two words isn't it: the ability to sustain. English is a dreadful language. We have the ability to sustain new behaviours through coaching, and that's what Continue & Begin Fast Coaching does.

So let's just summarise, the NDK Performance Model: we have explicit standards, ways of operating, expectations of how people will perform. We've got to have them delivered consistently, in all parts of our operation – not just some, not just most, but all parts of the organisation have to operate to these high levels.

And the third part of the NDK Performance Model is … to keep it alive, so it's not just something we did once. It's sustained and we keep it going every day, every week, every month, every quarter, every year, with every service-user, with every employee, and we do that through fast coaching the Continue & Begin way. And that's what you're going to learn on this programme.

## NDK Performance Model (family, health and well-being, education, community)

Ok, so outside of workplace organisations, either commercial, public sector or voluntary sector, we can use the NDK Performance Model, in a different way.

Organisations are usually – not always – pretty good at mapping out what they expect of their employees. The explicit standards may not be perfectly defined, and there may be some ambiguity in there, but for the most part the employee has an idea of what is expected of him.

This is not always – or even often – the case in families, in healthcare, in community groups or in education. This is problematic. Why? Because if we don't have an explicitly described set of standards – *specific* standards, *specific* ambitions, *specific* expectations or whatever else you want to call them – it's pretty difficult for the coachee to know if she is delivering on them.

This is where it gets really interesting, because there is very little in the way of explicit standards, ambitions or aspirations in relation to that tricky business of *How to Live.*

So, how to proceed? Well, we're going to have to make some, aren't we!

In many family scenarios, for example, where help has been asked for or has been imposed, there is a common theme: lack of structure or framework – the absence of unclear rules and clarity of expectation.

I remember a friend, Roger, coming to see me at my home to chat about a sports club we were involved with. Roger was an educational welfare officer due for retirement. He had experienced plenty of challenging families in his career. At the time, our house had – still has – a long entrance porch, around 15 metres long, attached to the side of the main property. It's where our four children kept their bicycles, surf boards, fishing rods, skating gear and all the collection of items adolescents and teenagers gather around them.

There were plenty of shoes … plenty! Shoes, wellies, soccer and rugby boots, shin pads, trainers, horse-riding boots, ski boots, surf boots, body boarding flippers, roller skates, school shoes, flip flops, slippers, formal shoes and masses of other assorted footwear. On top of that little lot my wife Claire had her own 'substantial' collection of shoes and boots and I had a few items of footwear myself. This had the potential for mayhem!

We had shelving made, the complete length of the porch. It went on forever, at different heights – low down at one end, for our youngest child, and gradually, along the length of the porch wall, getting higher for each older child, finishing up with higher shelving for Claire and myself. Each level of shelving had a wooden sign, painted: Rosie; George; Mart; Rob; Mum; Dad.

It was our way for establishing some form of order. The children – and Mum and Dad – were expected to place their shoes and boots in their allocated space; it was a family 'rule': put your shoes on the shelf please.

It was Roger's first visit to our home. 'Your kids will be alright,' he said.
'Why's that Rog?'
'Organised. They've got order. They'll be fine.'

It is essential, if coaching of behaviour is to work, for the coachee – the family member, the community member, the resident or the healthcare patient – to have a set of reference points to assess themselves against.

If they're not already in place it makes sense to help the individual develop a framework of ambitions, rules, standards, for them to refer to.

So, if we want to coach effectively, outside of an *organised organisation*, we may need first to help create the reference points for the individual, or group of individuals, to use.

Welfare workers, family workers, healthcare practitioners, teaching professionals and others working in communities – this is where the development of rules, standards and ambitions becomes a key activity, in advance of coaching.

That's the reality of it: we can't coach effectively without reference points.

## Coaching versus training or teaching

Ok, there is a difference between training, or teaching, and coaching. Let me explain what that difference is – it's just my model of the world, and I think it's the right one. It goes like this: training is about learning new skills, new processes, new knowledge, new behaviours. What's the common word? Yes, *new*. So training is about introducing people to new ideas, new concepts, new skills, new behaviours, new processes. It's different to coaching.

Remember from earlier, everything that you ever learned, everything you've ever experienced, every course you've ever been on, every book you've ever read, every experience you've had – you've seen, smelled, tasted, felt – everything is in here [points to back of head]. It's locked away in your own conscious mind – everything that ever happened. Maybe from time to time, maybe you're doing the washing up or just reflecting and suddenly something pops into your mind, a memory from years ago – that's right – and you think: 'Crikey, where did that come from?' Well, because it's always been there; everything you've learned is already filed away.

The challenge for some of the people you're going to be coaching is all the stuff they learned – it's all in there, it's still in there – it's just that they've forgotten to remember. It's still in there but they're having difficulty accessing it, and what we're doing coaching is... we help people remember the things that they've forgotten. That thing, that piece of knowledge, is still filed away in their unconscious mind, and we can help them find it again.

And we do that by using fantastic questions. We can help people re-access the things that they learned so that they can turn their learning into behaviour – *now* – and then keep that behaviour going.

So that's the difference between training and coaching.

Now let's just consider a couple of other things as well: mentoring and counselling. Let's just be clear on the difference between these things.

Mentoring is about finding somebody who's fantastic at a given skill or process or behaviour, and asking them to transfer some of their knowledge or experience to you. It often involves a degree of teaching or suggesting by the mentor.

Often the best person to mentor you is not someone in a position of influence in your life, maybe not even in your organisation, whatever your organisation may be. Perhaps the best person to mentor you is somebody outside of your everyday life. This could be helpful, because if they're outside of your immediate world then there's none of the emotional or relationship baggage that comes with bearing your soul to your boss, your family or your teacher. Mentors are fantastic because they've already been there – seen it and done it – and they can help you and guide you without relationship matters clouding your thinking – or their thinking.

Mentoring is not coaching. It's a different thing altogether.

And finally, counselling. We are not … or so far as I'm aware, and maybe one or two or you are, but there are not many psychoanalysts working outside of therapy and healthcare. If you're not in that world, if you don't have those skills, if you're not a psychotherapist or trained counsellor, then you're not really in a position where you can offer counselling, are you?

Continue & Begin Fast Coaching stays within safe parameters and, because of that, it can be used in the clumsiest of hands. We're not here to get into deep, heavy things with employees, students, family or community members or anybody else who you're *coaching*.

So, please remember Continue & Begin Fast Coaching is a coaching model – it's not a training model, it's not a mentoring model and it's certainly not a counselling model.

It's about helping people re-access the thing they already know – it's just that they forgot to remember. And it can be used by even the clumsiest of people to create fantastic personal change. That's Continue & Begin Fast Coaching.

## What makes a great coach?

Ok, let's think about what makes a great coach. What kind of attributes or characteristics make for a fantastic coach? In your workbook you'll see that there are a number of ideas I've already suggested to you: things like being an attentive listener; things like being empathetic; like being a precision questioner. All these are attributes and characteristics that I think help people operate skilfully in their role as a coach.

Now, we're going to ask you to take a pen and write down as many attributes you can think of: what makes a great coach? I've given you three already. I think you can make at least 20. Don't evaluate too much, just take that consciousness and allow it to stream itself down onto that piece of paper: as many as you can, at least 20. Off you go.

| | | | |
|---|---|---|---|
| attentive listener | | | |
| empathetic | | | |
| precision questioner | | | |
| | | | |
| | | | |

## English is Rubbish – specificity of meaning

Alright then, so we've got a big list. I'm hoping you could get at least 20 attributes of a great coach on your big list. Let's just identify one or two that you've written down.

Maybe you put down things like being approachable. Maybe you have said that being a great communicator helps in the process of being a great coach. Maybe you talk about the willingness to be flexible as an attribute of a great coach. Here's my question for you: if you've written down 'being approachable', what do you mean by that, specifically? Help me to understand – help yourself to understand – what specifically do you mean by that? Being approachable?

Let's take some of the other phrases that I suggested: being a great communicator. What does that mean specifically? What do you mean by that phrase: being a great communicator. Help me to understand. Or maybe you've said 'be flexible'. Well, in what way, specifically, do you mean 'be flexible'? I don't understand. Help me to understand. Be more specific and precise please.

Why am I asking you these questions? Well, because English is Rubbish.

Now I have to say, most languages are rubbish. We've only been using spoken language – well the scientists tell us anyway – for about 100,000 years, and we're still not very good at it. And certainly English, along with many other languages, is full of ambiguities and generalisations – words and phrases that can be interpreted in lots of different ways.

So part of the role of being a fantastic workplace coach, or social coach, or community health coach, sports coach or a family coach is what? What are the secrets to success? It's to ask fantastic questions to gain specificity of meaning, and we do that by asking fabulous questions to really understand what the other person means. English is Rubbish!

## Six and three

Now, let's just go back to that list of the 20 attributes of a great coach. Here's what I'd like you to do: in your workbook you'll see a list; there are two columns – one that says Six and the other says Three. What I'd like you to do is to think about yourself and your role as a coach.

What are you really good at, already? What are you already really talented at? Look back through that list of 20 attributes and identify six of those things that you can say – hand on your heart – you're already really, really good at in your role as a coach. Write it down under the heading Six in your workbook and then – and only then – wallow in your success, feel good about the fantastic skill that you've already got as a coach.

And then, when you are feeling good and your ego is strong, now look back through the list and ask yourself, 'Can I identify two or three of these coaching attributes that I know maybe I could be a little bit better at?' and make a note of those as well.

Six things that you're already really skilful at – wallow in it, feel good – and then one, two, a maximum of three of those coaching skills that you think: 'You know, I could probably be a little bit better at that particular attribute'. Off you go, just a few minutes.

## Six and three responses

(Transcript extract from a Fast Coaching event)

**NDK**: Ok, volunteer please. Who would like to share their six and three?

**Agnieszka**: I will.

**NDK**: Ok, cool. Fire away Agnieszka.

**Agnieszka**: Well the three things I need to improve upon are, being more assertive …

**NDK**: Woah there Agnieszka! You've started with the three. Why did you do that?

**Agnieszka**: I don't know, I just did.

**NDK**: Hmmm … I noticed some of you began the six and three exercises by noting down the coaching attributes you want to get better at. That's quite common, some people do that. I wonder why that happens? You may be curious too … hmmm. Anyway, Agnieszka, let's start with the six shall we? What have you got? Take your time.

**Agnieszka**: Ok, er … I'm good at listening.

**NDK**: Excellent! So, what else are you good at?

**Agnieszka**: I've written here I'm quite good at being empathetic.

**NDK**: 'Quite good'! You know how to celebrate don't you Agnieszka!

[Laughter]

**NDK**; What else have you got there?

**Agnieszka**: Persistent.

**NDK**; What does that mean, specifically?

**Agnieszka**: That I don't let up on helping people. I keep checking they're ok.

**NDK**; Nice. Tell me some other things you're good at as a coach.

**Agnieszka**: I challenge people.

**NDK**; Oh, yeah? How specifically do you do that?

**Agnieszka**: I remind them of what they said they would do, and challenge them if they are not doing it.

**NDK**; That's impressive. What else?

**Agnieszka**: I like to ask people what they're thinking.

**NDK**; What? Get inside their world? See things from their perspective? Understand what's happening in their mind? That wouldn't be helpful to you would it, surely?

[Laughter]

**NDK**; That is really cool Agnieszka, very cool indeed. There's something else in your mind, about the things you do really well when you're coaching.

**Agnieszka**: I smile, to put people at ease.

**NDK**; Oh yeah? Why do you want them at ease then?

**Agnieszka**: Because people will only open up to you if you have a rapport with them. It's important to gain their trust.

**NDK**; Ok, I'm with you. Anything else on your six list?

**Agnieszka**: No that's it.

**NDK**: Alright then. So, very quickly, run through the list of six, really quickly. In your role as a coach you're good at what specifically?

**Agnieszka**: Listening, being empathetic, being persistent, I challenge people, I ask them what they're thinking, oh and I smile at them.

**NDK**: Wow! How about that! That's impressive, really impressive. You must be really pleased with that list? Are you?

**Agnieszka**: I suppose so, yeah.

**NDK**: Alright! When was the last time you really celebrated how talented you are at something?

**Agnieszka**: A long time ago. Maybe never. Maybe before an interview or something.

**NDK**: Ok. And how does it feel now you've recognised how skilled and talented you are at coaching?

**Agnieszka**: Yes, good, it feels nice.

**NDK**: Quite right too, that's an impressive list. You're already brilliant, you can leave now. No need for you to do this course.

[Laughter]

**NDK**: Now, I guess you'd like to continue to do those brill things when you're coaching people, is that right?

**Agnieszka**: Of course.

**NDK**: Splendid. So, now you've realised just how good you are at this coaching business, can you think of a few things that would make you even better, even more skilled and effective than you already are? I think you may have written a few ideas down?

[Laughter]

**Agnieszka**: Yes Nick, I have!

[Laughter]

**NDK**: Well ok then Agnieszka, please share them with us!

**Agnieszka**: I'd like to be better at being assertive.

**NDK**: In what way specifically?

**Agnieszka**: Well, when I challenge someone I feel a bit nervous about what they're going to say, like if they're going to be aggressive to me or something.

**NDK**: Ok, understood. We're not getting into the 'how' right now. We're just identifying areas to work on, ok? What else have you got there?

**Agnieszka**: Questioning. Don't think I'm very good at asking the right questions. I could do with some new ideas.

**NDK**: Ok, that's fine. I'm sure that's something you can develop with time and maybe a little guidance. Tell me something else you'd like to become even better at as a coach?

**Agnieszka**: Note taking. When I meet up with someone – I don't know, say a week later – I've forgotten what we've talked about. I think I should take more notes, but I'm not sure how to do it without it looking like I'm getting all formal with them, if that makes sense.

**NDK**: It makes absolute sense Agnieszka. Thank you. Anything else?

**Agnieszka**: No, that's it.

**NDK**: Ok, great we have a really useful developmental list there, things that will help you become even more talented than you already are as a coach, is that right?

**Agnieszka**: Yes.

**NDK**: Excellent. And what are the things you want to develop? Run through them super-quick.

**Agnieszka**: Be better at being assertive.

**NDK** (interrupts): Are you sure?

**Agnieszka**: Yes!

[Laughter]

**NDK**: Aha! Ok, and …?

**Agnieszka**: Questioning and note taking.

**NDK**: Alright, so how will that make you feel, when you're continuing to do all those good things, and now you're being assertive, asking super-effective questions, and you're also making notes to help you prepare for follow-up coaching sessions. How will you feel when you're doing that?

**Agnieszka**: Amazing. I'd feel wonderful, really good, like I was a proper professional coach.

**NDK**: Cool! And you'd like that would you?

**Agnieszka**. Very much please. Can you arrange that for me please Nick?

[Laughter]

**NDK**: I'm guessing there are some things that have to happen in order for you to do those things, right? Things like finding out some good questioning techniques, learning about assertion, getting a note book and pen, that kind of thing?

[Laughter]

**Agnieszka**: Ha! Yes, I will have to do some research. Of course, yes.

**NDK**: And are you committed to doing these new things? Or have you just being humouring us all for the purposes of this activity? Are you serious about making these changes?

**Agnieszka**: I am, actually, very serious. It's something I want to do and I'm going to.

**NDK**: That's fantastic, thank you Agnieszka. Let's have a round of applause for Agnieszka, that's right. Thank you, Agnieszka.

[Applause]

**NDK**: Ladies and gentlemen, what you've experienced there is a very simple example of Continue & Begin Fast Coaching. It's not the full approach and there are things we might like to add. For the moment though, recognise how simple and quick that was. Time wise, how long did it take?

**Jonathan**: About 5 minutes?

**NDK**: Something like that – 5, maybe 6, maybe 4. Not long anyway. Continue & Begin Fast Coaching is fast. We don't need an hour, or even half an hour. We don't need a therapist's couch and have the coachee lay there with dribble dripping off her chin. It's fast and it makes people feel good. Would you like to know how to do it?

**Audience**: Yes!

**NDK**: Ok, well pay attention then!

[Laughter]

## Surface structure, deep structure, experience
(Transcript extract from a Fast Coaching event)

**NDK**: Ok, who's had a long drive here today?

**Michelle**: I have.

**NDK**: Tell us about your journey.

**Michelle**: It was ok. Got stuck on the ring road though.

**NDK** writes on flipchart: It was ok. Got stuck on the ring road though.

**NDK**: What time did you leave home Michelle?

**Michelle**: 6.45

**NDK**: Did you come by car?

**Michelle**: Yes.

**NDK** Did you drive or were you a passenger?

**Michelle**: I drove.

**NDK**: Were you alone in the car?

**Michelle**: Yes.

**NDK**: Where was your car parked?

**Michelle**: On my drive.

**NDK**: Facing your home or facing away from your home?

**Michelle**: Facing my home.

**NDK**: What sort of car is it?

**Michelle**: It's a VW Golf.

**NDK** Ok, colour?

**Michelle**: Red.

**NDK**: 4-door or 2-door?

**Michelle**: 4-door.

**NDK**: Is your driveway level or on a slope?

**Michelle**: Bit of a slope actually, up towards the garage door.

**NDK**: You've got a garage door! You never mentioned that!

**Michelle**: You didn't ask!

[Laughter]

**NDK**: Ok, well I suppose you reversed out of your drive?

**Michelle**: Yes.

**NDK**: Onto a side road? A main road? A cul-de-sac?

**Michelle**: It's quite a busy road.

**NDK**: Much traffic about this morning?

**Michelle**: Kind of. There's roadworks and temporary traffic lights.

**NDK**: Ok. Was there music playing in your car?

**Michelle**: Yes.

**NDK**: Radio? CD?

**Michelle**: Off my phone.

**NDK**: Ok. What was the music?

**Michelle**: All sorts, I had it on shuffle.

**NDK**: Ok, thanks Michelle. And ladies and gentlemen, we haven't even started the journey yet. What was the question I asked Michelle? Who remembers?

**Stephen**: 'Tell us about your journey.'

**NDK**: Correct. And what was Michelle's response to that question? It's written here!

**Audience members**: 'It was ok. Got stuck on the ring road though.'

**NDK**: Correct. Michelle's response was what's called a surface structure utterance. It's the initial response. It was an overview of what she thought was relevant information. Who has children? [Hands raised] Little children? Or maybe you remember when they were little children? [Hands raised]

Do you remember when they first went to school? How excited they were when they told you all about their day? All that detail? I remember collecting my daughter Rosie from school when she was little. She was maybe 5 or 6 years old. I asked her what she had done at school that day.

'Well Daddy, I was playing with Charlotte in the playground and we were skipping and then Megan and Savannah came and we played chase and Harriett fell over and hurt her knee really badly and we had to find a teacher and then ...' and the story went on and on '... and the bell went for the **start** of school ... and then ...'

Rosie hadn't learned about information overview or conciseness; she was so excited by the detail.

Anyone got teenagers? Or remembers when your kids were adolescents and teenagers? [Hands raised]

It's a bit different with older children isn't it? [Laughter] Try the same question with a 14-year-old and it's a different response.

'What did you do at school today?'

'Nothing.'

'You must have done something.'

'English.'

'Oh, ok, how was it?'

'Alright.'

It's tough work! Some adolescents and teenagers have learned to delete vast amounts of detail in order to minimise their response content.

Take a look at this iceberg image in your workbook. It describes three levels of communication. In the bottom section we have the experience, the meaning or the feeling the person has in mind. Next up the iceberg is what's called the *deep structure* of language: the words, the vocabulary that the individual has at their disposal, the relevant words they can choose to use, or not use, to communicate meaning, experience or feeling. And the top section is the *surface structure*, the utterance which the individual chooses to use in communicating meaning.

For Michelle it was: 'It was ok. Got stuck on the ring road though.' For Rosie it was a lengthy description of all the details of her experiences before school had even started. For the teenager it was a one word answer, offering the minimum possible response.

When we get a *surface structure* utterance in a coaching context we have an impoverished representation of the coachee's experience, their meaning or feeling. It is vital we find out more. And we do that by asking really good questions. Would you like to find out more about what type of questions we can ask?

## Delete, distort, generalise

So, *surface structure*, *deep structure*, experience, meaning and feeling. Let's explore some more about how coachees communicate. Incidentally, this is about how *we* communicate as well.

*Deletion* in our communication is something we all do. We delete parts of the full message, just like Michelle did: 'It was ok. Got stuck on the ring road though.' Everyone deletes detail. We have to, to get through the day. Have a look in your workbook and look at the *deletion* examples described there.

*Distortion* is another way we cause difficulties with our communication. We make assumptions, sometimes making massive leaps in faith, guessing at meaning or reading something into a situation that may or may not be true. Sometimes we select a meaning from a set of circumstances. This can cause real difficulties if the assumptions we make are not accurate. Have a look here in the workbook at some examples.

And the final type of miscommunication we can experience from coachees and which we all use is *generalisation*. We all do it ladies and gentlemen. We make sweeping comments about a class of ideas and make broad statements that are rarely accurate in all circumstances. *Generalisation* is a way of making a collective idea from a multitude of individual ideas. It's a very dangerous thing to do! Check out the examples in the workbook.

So when we listen to a coachee we can be aware she is using language with limited accuracy. We know she is using *surface structure* utterances; we know she has a deeper vocabulary available to describe her meaning; and we know she is habitually (that's *habit*-ually) deleting, distorting and generalising as she speaks to us.

Not as simple as we thought is it?

If we are to gain specificity of language – and therefore accuracy of meaning – it is essential we help the coachee by asking targeted questions that will reveal greater accuracy and detail. There are some good *specificity questions* described there in the workbook. We're going to learn other techniques today which will help you do that with elegance. Interested?

## What else? vs Anything else?

Ok, let's go back to the list you made of six and three. Or maybe you ended up with five and two, or four and two – or something like that; it doesn't matter. So, you've got a big old list of things you're proud of, parts of your role that you're already really, really good at. Now, these are your *continue to*'s, because I'm guessing you'd like to continue to do those things well in your role as a coach, and you've identified just a few things that you want to *begin to* work on, to do differently perhaps, to allow yourself to become even better in your role as a coach.

Now this is in essence Continue & Begin. We identify from the coachee a fabulous list of things that they're good at, things that maybe they haven't thought about for a while, to help them recognise just how skilful they already are. And when the skill levels are identified, the ego, the self-image, the self-worth, the self-esteem become stronger.

And the truism is this, that when people are feeling confident about themselves they're much more likely to take on opportunities to develop and grow as a person. A coachee is much more likely to take on those challenges when they're feeling strong already. Compare that to someone who's feeling a little low in self-confidence; how likely they are to feel enthusiastic about growing and developing – no!

Much better to help people feel fantastic about themselves, then they can aspire to even greater things. That's what we do in Continue & Begin: we identify a lot of *continue to*'s and just a few *begin to*'s.

So, in the process of doing this we're going to ask people some questions, the kind of questions that tease out some of those *continue to*'s and identify just a few of the *begin to*'s.

Here's the thing: most people are pretty good at identifying the *begin to*'s – the improvement criteria they're already focused on – what they're

**bad** at. When you were doing the six and three activity just now, some of you started with the three, didn't you? Now why was that then? Some folk go straight for self-flagellation. Weirdos! It's understandable really, some people just love beating themselves up. Well here's the news guys – many of you have been doing that for a long time; you're very good at criticising yourself. Well time's up! You've done enough of that. And anyway, the best thing about the past is, it's over.

Our role as Continue & Begin coaches is to help people *feel good*.

How do we do it? Well, we use two types of questions and if you have a look in your workbook you'll see those two questions described. Let's have a look at the first one; the first one is: 'What else?'

Now this question 'What else?' is a special type of question; it's called a presupposition. That's a fancy phrase that's a nominalisation of a verb. What's the verb? The verb is to *presuppose.*

What does the question 'What else?' presuppose? Well, of course, it presupposes there is something else to think about. 'What else are you pleased with?'; 'What else did you do well?'

It presupposes that there *is* something else! Why is this significant? Well, because when we ask firm, assertive questions using a presupposition such as 'What else? Tell me some other things', when we ask those questions the unconscious mind responds in the coachee. And now, this is a truism: most people know about the unconscious mind, all those things that are stored away. And I've got to tell you folks, the unconscious mind is fantastic at some things: it's wonderful at looking after what's called your *autonomic nervous system.*

Autonomic nervous system? What is *that?* Well it's the thing that looks after your heart rate, it looks after your breathing, looks after your sweating, blinking – all those kinds of things. It's the reason why we don't have to wake up at night every 20 seconds to say, 'Surely it's time for me to draw another breath'. We don't need to do that because the autonomic nervous system does it for us.

But apart from that it will do *nothing* if it can get away with it; it's bone idle. The autonomic nervous system is fantastic at just a few survival things, but if we don't give it a firm instruction it will be like a lazy teenager –

you know, sat at home head down in the phone and eating pizza. It'll do nothing, it's lazy ... so we have to give a firm instruction. 'What else are you pleased with? Tell me some other things you've done well?' Then the unconscious mind will sit up and take action. The kind of language you use will determine how receptive and responsive the autonomic nervous system is in the unconscious mind.

Compare the question 'What else?' with this question: 'Anything else?' Remember, the unconscious mind is lazy. Give it a chance to do nothing, it will do nothing.

'Anything else that you're pleased with?' What's the response likely to be? 'I can't think of anything, no not really'.

So the *power* of the questions we ask during the coaching process – to tease out all of those *continue to*'s, and to tease out a few *begin to*'s – is absolutely critical.

'What else?' versus 'Anything else?' They are two very profoundly different questions. One demands an answer, the other invites your coachee's unconscious mind to go back to social media and the pizza slices.

## Movement or motivation?

Let's have a think about motivation and the kind of things that help people get excited about making changes to their lives, whether it's at work, at home in the family, in education or maybe something to do with health.

There was a psychologist back in the sixties and seventies called Fred Herzberg, and Herzberg did a lot of work on what gets people motivated. He identified something that he called KITA, K-I-T-A, it's a little bit rude; it means Kick – In – The – Bottom, and what he said was, there are two types of KITAs. There are negative KITAs: threats, punishments, criticism, those kinds of things – and the worst kind of negative KITA, the withdrawal of 'love', in whatever context that might be.

Positive KITAs are incentives, rewards, cash prizes, those kinds of things, and what Fred said was that we can get people to *move*, through the use of a KITA – either a negative or positive. We can get people to *do things*. They may not want to do it, but they'll do it; we can get movement.

KITA

Now, let me give you an example. I need a volunteer … yes, you'll do nicely.

So, my car is outside my house right now and I'm going to tell you it's filthy – and I mean really dirty – and it needs a proper clean, a proper valet, inside and out. What I would like you to do is – and it should only take you 2 or 3 hours – is to come round to my house and clean my car for me. Would you? I live on the Isle of Wight, in England by the way … yes, yes, I know it's a bit of a trek for you. I realise there's a bit a travelling time for you. Well, ok, yes – rather a lot of travelling time, yes. Anyway, if you would do that for me, that would be very kind. Would you like to do that please? Or … you'd prefer not? Oh.

What about if I was to offer you some form of reward – I mean a serious reward. If I was to say, in the back of my car there are tens of thousands of pounds and you can have it all if you come and give my car a clean for a couple of hours. Maybe you'd feel a little differently. You would? Oh that's lovely, thank you. And yes, tomorrow would be fine.

You see, I can get you to do it. Do you want to do it? No. But I can get you to *move*. Movement is different to motivation.

What if I want you to move again? If I want you to clean my car again in the future? What have I got to do? I've got to give you some more reward, some more cash or maybe some fear, some nasty threat – or some punishment.

Do you want to do it? No. But will you do it? Yes.

Movement is different to motivation. Motivation is when it comes from inside; when people are passionate about things; when they want to do it because – they want to do it. That's motivation.

And one of the great things about Continue & Begin Fast Coaching is we can help people to celebrate the things they're already doing well – to make them feel good, to get their ego strong, to make them feel fantastic about their skills, because when people are feeling fantastic about themselves they're much more likely to take on opportunities to perform to *even higher* levels.

That's why Continue & Begin is so powerful; not only is it quick, but it makes people feel fantastic, so they have a passion and a drive to do *even better*. Their motivation comes through and we don't have to apply any KITAs at all; they will do it because they will want to do it – because they feel good about challenge and aspiration.

That's the difference between movement and motivation.

## Observation or judgement?

So, let's have a think about the nature of language and the kind of ways we phrase things when we're making a coaching comment on someone's performance.

There's a difference between what I call *observation* comments and *judgemental* comments. Let's just explore this.

So in a customer-facing workplace environment a comment may be a judgemental comment if it's something along these lines: 'When that customer asked for directions you weren't very helpful, you weren't very interested in helping her, were you, Julia?'

Observation or judgement?

This is judgemental; this is some form of criticism, an opinion, a verdict on someone's performance – almost a mind-read: 'You weren't interested in helping her, were you?' Can you hear the mind-read?

'You weren't interested, were you?'

This is judgemental. It's not helping us in the process of people celebrating the things they're doing well – and *begin to* do some things differently and *even better*.

Now, let's compare that language pattern with something that is observational – an observation of truth, something that happens. So first of all let's just test it again: 'When that customer asked for directions you weren't very helpful, you weren't interested in helping her, were you?'

Can you hear the verdict, the opinion, the mind-reading – and also the tone and the physiology that goes with that?

Now let's compare it with the observation approach, which is offering the same opportunity to explore but in a different, more friendly and constructive way. We might go like this: 'When that customer asked for directions I noticed you didn't walk with her to the information point. What were you thinking about at that moment there?'

Hear the difference? Judgemental and observation: one is a verdict, criticism – a mind-read of what you were thinking or the other person was thinking. The other is an observation of fact: the things that we've seen and heard. There is a difference between those two.

Judgemental comments get people's backs up; they create resistance inside them and sometimes confrontation and argument. Observations don't do those things. Observations are just statements of things that you've seen and heard. And as we progress through Continue & Begin Fast Coaching you'll recognise that observational comments are really, really, helpful for stimulating discussion. Judgement comments get people's backs up. We don't want to do that; we want to make people feel good.

Judgements ... observations. In your workbook you'll see a list of comments, and the opportunity's there for you to identify if that comment is an observation – a fact, just a straight stimulus for conversation – or is it some form of criticism, judgement, opinion, verdict or mind-read in the form of a judgemental comment.

Read down through those questions and ask yourself is it a J for Judgement? Or an O for Observation? Enjoy the exercise.

The following exercise is from a family coaching version of Continue & Begin Fast Coaching:

1. 'When Jamie was talking to you about his toys, you weren't interested in him.'
   Judgement or observation?

2. 'I heard you with Jade in the kitchen. You were angry.'
   Judgement or observation?

3. 'When your mum asked you to fetch a towel you said, "Get it yourself."'
   Judgement or observation?

4. 'I noticed earlier today you brought your dirty clothes down to the kitchen, put them in the washing machine and turned it on.'
   Judgement or observation?

5. 'When Charlotte started shouting, you did really well.'
   Judgement or observation?

6. 'You just can't be bothered, can you?'
   Judgement or observation?

7. 'You were out of bed by 7.30, made breakfast for the children with toast and jam, and you made sure Mathew and Tanya were both dressed in clean uniform and ready for school by 8.15.'
   Judgement or observation?

8. 'You did a good job when the arguing started.'
   Judgement or observation?

Aright, so we've been down through those statements there and you've identified whether those comments were observational statements of fact or whether they were judgements, verdicts, opinions or mind-reading. Down through that list you may have come across one or more that were what I call *chocolate praise* – they're nice judgement phrases such as: 'You did really well there. Well done, that was nice.'

Now, *chocolate praise* feels good; 'Well done,' feels good, but they're temporary in their impact. We all like getting a pat on the back from time to time don't we? It feels nice but here's the challenge: it doesn't last long and – perhaps more importantly – it doesn't help us to understand precisely what it is that we did that made our performance so good.

It's a nice judgement, but it's not helpful. I call it *chocolate praise* because – just like when you eat a piece of chocolate – the blood sugar level goes up, but not for long; it comes crashing down again pretty quickly. This is why some people eat lots of chocolate to see if they can stay up there. Well, it works for a while – but it has repercussions.

Alright, so *chocolate praise* makes us feel good, but it's doesn't help us understand what I call the Structure of Well-Done-Ness – the building blocks of excellence that make someone's performance so outstanding.

If we were to be really effective workplace coaches, a community coach, sports coach, any form of coach, a family coach, then it's really important we help the coachee recognise for themselves those building blocks, the Lego bricks, the key things that happened that made their performance so good.

And the way that we do that is by asking fantastic questions related to ... do you remember ...? The NDK Performance Model: the bottom piece, the explicit standards or agreed aspirations. If we can help people to identify for themselves the things that they did, that fit with those explicit standards or agreed aspirations, if we could help them to recognise which part of those things they've done well *now* ... *now* they are starting to understand the structure of their excellence, and in a moment I'm going to tell you a story to illustrate just that.

## Chocolate praise

CHOCOLATE PRAISE

Well anyway, let's just explore this with an example shall we?

I was working at home some years ago – quite a long while ago – and I was doing some work in my study, and in through the front door came

Number Two Son. When you've got a lot of children, you have to give them numbers.

So in came Number Two Son, and he was supposed to be at school doing his A levels. He had a wetsuit on and he had a surfboard and he'd clearly been enjoying himself in the sea. I said:

'What's going on Martin? Shouldn't you be at school?'

'I've got a free period.'

Well, as it turns out, the A levels these days … well, crikey you could cram the whole two years into about two weeks, there are so many free periods. Anyway, I said to him, 'Martin, how are you getting on at school anyway, son?'

'Alright.'

Remember what we were saying earlier about *deletion* and *generalisation* in language?

'What do you mean by "alright" specifically? Have you had any grades back?'

'Yeah.'

Pulling teeth, this was: 'Which grades specifically? For what subjects Martin?'

'Physics.'

'Oh right, how did you get on?'

'Alright.'

'Got any coursework back?'

'Yeah.'

'Can I see it?'

'S'pose so.'

Well, he went to his room and he came back and he put the assignment on my desk – the physics assignment – and on it, it said: '(A) Well done!'

Hmmm … I'm an experienced father: 'Who wrote that Martin?'

'Woody.' (Aha! Were my suspicions right?)

'Who's Woody?'

'Mr Woods, the physics teacher.'

'Oh, well, fair enough. Well, why did he write (A)? What was it that you did to get an A?'

'I dunno, because it's good.'

'Yes but why specifically? What was it that you did that caused him to write (A)? What was it about your piece of work that was so special?'

'I don't know, do I?'

'You'd better find out then!'

Well, the next day Martin came home again and he said, 'Yo Dad, I saw Woody.'

'Who? Oh yes! How did you get on?'

'Really good. The reason I got an A was … well, he gave us a mathematical formula to calculate and I got that right, but the real reason was he gave us a process to follow – a kind of a structure for the presentation of the piece of work. He wanted a front page, he wanted a contents page, he wanted acknowledgements, he wanted the methodology, he wanted the introduction, the findings, the conclusion – and he wanted the whole thing presented in a certain way and I'd done that. And what he said to me was, if I did the same thing for the next piece of coursework the chances are I'll get another A.'

'Ah, Martin that's fantastic! You've just learned the Structure of Well-Done-Ness for physics A-level assignments! You now know how to put the coursework information together in such a way that you're almost certainly going to get another A. You understand the structure of excellence for a physics A-level assignment.'

'Epic, Dad.'

Epic indeed. You see, in the process of coaching it's critical that we help our coachee, the person we're coaching. It's critical that we help them to understand the component parts, the elements, the building blocks that form their excellence, when they put the little Lego bricks together, the little behaviours and processes and activities that made their performance so good: Their Structure of Well-Done-Ness.

Their Structure of Well-Done-Ness components are the really powerful *continue to*'s – the ones that are self-identified – in relation to a set of explicit standards or agreed aspirations.

Because the alternative is to give them a 'Well Done', to give them a piece of chocolate, which makes them feel good for a little while – but it's not sustainable.

STRUCTURE OF WELL·DONE·NESS

And we already know that the secret to success in personal behaviour is to have explicit standards or agreed aspirations that describe a stated excellence. If the coachee is to deliver that excellence consistently and sustain it every day, every week, every month, every year – to keep the plates spinning, to keep the momentum going – it is absolutely essential we help people to understand their Structure of Well-Done-Ness and not just give them a 'Well Done'. It's just *chocolate praise*.

Incidentally, Martin went on to gain a first in Renewables Engineering at the University of Exeter.

## The But Monster

Ok, so we talked just now about judgemental comments, and what we're going to do now is explore some other language patterns that cause damage, that get in the way of an effective coaching process. So let's just run through this.

Here's the first one, so listen carefully to the language pattern: 'Now, er ... you've done well on the coursework so far, working through the workbook, and some of the things that you've written down have been, er … [downward inflection in voice] well, they've been helpful.'

What word is coming? What is it I'm about to say? Yes, you know intuitively. You understand the next word is going to be 'But …'

Let's run it again: 'Well you've … you've done well … and, er … some of the things you've written down [downward inflection in voice] have been helpful.' You just know the next word is going to be 'But', don't you? How did you know? Well you know because of the tonality of my voice; you know because of the physiology that I'm illustrating with my facial expression, my breathing patterns and everything else. And you've heard and experienced these types of communicating many times in the past, haven't you? You know that the next word that's coming out is going to be a 'But'.

Now, what's coming after the 'But'? You know, you understand. Intuitively you know the next thing is going to be some form of criticism, some form of request for change, some form of negative vibe and you're getting ready for it.

Let's check that again: 'You've done some good things this morning, and one or two of the things you've written in your workbook have been [downward inflection] helpful.'

You know a 'But' is coming, and you know that after the 'But' is going to be some request for change. It's what I call the But Monster and it's coming to bite you on the bum!

The BUT Monster

The But Monster – what is does – it stops people from feeling good. It gets them ready for some impending pain, which is absolutely *not* what we want to do for Continue & Begin Fast Coaching. Remember we want people to feel good. If you start to use the word 'But', all of those natural downward inflections in the voice – all of the physiology and tonality – it gives the game away before you even say the word 'But' and then the request for change.

So my guidance to you is this: remove the But Monster from your coaching vocabulary. Change the way you help people to change. If you want them to operate in a different way, use a different way of communicating.

There is a great way of operating: instead of using the But Monster we use the word 'And'. We keep the tonality up, we keep the facial expressions and everything else about body language really positive. Here it goes: 'Hey, some of the things you've done this morning working through the workbook and notes are fantastic – you've done some great stuff, and what would be really great as we progress is if you could also ...'

You're hearing this: there is a still a request for change and instead of the But Monster, there is an 'And'. You may not even have heard it – it was so slick. There is a difference between the But Monster and 'And'.

You can use a similar approach: instead of using 'And' we simply break the sentence into two with a full stop. Deep breath and swallow in the middle of the two ideas – current and future. Here it goes:

'Hey, some of the things you've done this morning working through the workbook and notes are fantastic – you've done some great stuff. [Full stop ... deep breath ... swallow.] What would be really great, as we progress, is if you could also ...'

Get the idea? We simply avoid the But Monster. It's a technique used extensively in therapeutic contexts, because some therapists know that 'But' can jolt a patient out of feelings of comfort and relaxation – it creates anxiety – and we don't want our Continue & Begin Fast Coaching coachees feeling anxious. Anxiety is an inhibitor to learning.

## Should-ing and must debators

Now, there are other language patterns that get in the way of helping people feel good; here is one of them: 'What you must do ... what you need to do … what you should do … what you've got to do … what you ought to do …'

In these language patterns you can almost see and hear the finger pointing. Let's run it again: 'What you need to do … what you should do … what you have to do … what you ought to do … what you've got to do …'

These are confrontational, aggressive, condescending, bullying language patterns that put people on the back foot. *Should*-ing is particularly annoying for coachees. Poorly skilled coaches – and too many mentors by the way – *should* all over their coachees.

I have an old rugby teammate I enjoy a beer with: Jeff. We meet up every now and again for an evening of nostalgia and reminiscing about Glory Days, When We Were Kings, that sort of thing – harmless evenings of delusion, you know. I used to knock on his door and say, 'I have beer tokens in my pocket! Would you like to come and spend them with me?' and Jeff would grab his coat and we'd be off.

Then he got married – for the third time. We'd had a conversation about it, obviously; he did it anyway. So then when I used to call for him you know – to come out to play – his new wife was there and she'd be asking about what I'd been doing at work, and I'd say : 'Well, I've been busy this week Charlotte, good fun. You know, a bit of UK, a bit of Europe.

Been with a client in Edinburgh; I was in Stuttgart on Wednesday and I've been doing some business in London.'

And then it would start: 'What you need to do Nick is do less travelling. You should spend less time at work at your age, you ought to be slowing down. You've got to think about your health – you should go part-time.'

She's a *should*-er!

So anyway, now I go straight to the pub and meet Jeff there.

In the context of Continue & Begin Fast Coaching *should*-ing doesn't help. Let's get rid of need to, should do, must, got to, have to – let's get rid of those phrases. They are not helping people to feel good.

*Should*-ers. They're everywhere. Be alert at all times.

## Other language that hurts

Right, so what other phrases get in the way when we're trying to build up a coachee's confidence and identify *even better* ways of operating? Ok, here's a few more to be wary of, alright?

'How many times have I told you this?'

This is not something conducive to making people feel good. What else have we got?

'I don't mean to criticise …' What word is coming next? You know don't you: it's the But Monster.

Well, what else have we got?

'You could have done so much better …'

Oh, right, well … thanks for being so encouraging, you moron.

Here's another one: 'If I were you …'

Yeah? Well you're not, so shut up.

These phrases just put people's backs up. It doesn't help a person feel good.

And what about the worst question in the world? It's this: 'Why can't you do it?'

Now let's just think about this: 'Why can't you do it?'

Do you remember earlier, the stuff about assertive statements and questions – the presuppositions? Yes you do remember it; it's in your mind. Where did you file it? Remember? Ok, here we go: 'What else? Tell me some other things.'

When we ask presupposition questions assertively, a person's unconscious mind will seek the answer to the question. When we ask somebody 'Why

can't you do it?' they go on a journey; there's a fancy phrases for it – it's called a transderivational search. It just means going through the filing cabinets of the mind until they find the reason why they can't do it.

And what happens is this: you ask them the question 'Why can't you do it? How many times have I got to tell you? Why can't you do it?' and they go through the search pattern, they find the reason why, and then it's presented to you – justifying the reason why they can't do it. What are you supposed to do then? 'Oh never mind, that's fine, I didn't realise.'

Noooo!

'Why can't you?' – it's a dreadful question.

Now, a bit later on, I'm going to introduce you to something called Can't to Can Belief Busting, which is just awesome. It's so much better than 'Why can't you?' It's is a fantastic way of helping people move from where they are to a change position, without any of these destructive language patterns I described to you just now. It builds massive motivation.

Would you like to know about Can't to Can Belief Busting? It's really awesome. You would? Well, you'll just have to wait a bit longer.

## The dangers of tell

'How many times do I have to tell you?' Heard that before? Maybe you heard it being said, or maybe you said it to someone? Oh no!

Come on though, I mean sometimes people have to be told so many times you wonder if they're actually listening – or are they just dim, right? Hmmm … well let's have a think about this, shall we?

When we use *tell* we're being 'teachy': it's didactic, it's an instructional way of getting a message across. In fact it's a really inefficient way of embedding new knowledge and expecting it to magically turn into behaviour that sticks. That's why you have to do it again and again. Because it's a rubbish way of changing people's behaviour – absolute rubbish.

*Tell* is a one-way street. *Tell* is trainer-driven: it's not learner-focused. *Tell* is about as far away from getting inside the learner's world as you can get. When we *tell* there is no ownership by the coachee, no personal responsibility, no inner search for solutions and choices, no referencing to explicitly described standards of performance. There's just a requirement to comply with rote learning. *Tell* is a personal development strategy built on assumption – an assumption that the coachee will comply with repeated instruction.

*Tell* is rubbish. In Continue & Begin Fast Coaching we encourage the coachee to reflect on her behaviour, to measure her behaviour against a set of explicit standards or agreed aspirations. The standards or aspirations are the reference points, the benchmarks.

This is why in Continue & Begin Fast Coaching we rarely, if ever, provide the answers. We may *nudge*, we may ask questions, we may refer to the explicit standards or agreed aspirations. We do not *tell*.

Continue & Begin Fast Coaching works so well because it encourages self-awareness and self-discovery.

## Constructive language patterns – opening lines

We have to get the ball rolling don't we? Start the process of fast coaching, get the coachee chatting and keeping the vibe positive and productive – maybe even enjoyable! What? Enjoyable? Are you mad? That would never work …

Of course it can. Continue & Begin is based on ego-strengthening and helping people celebrate their successes, no matter how small or insignificant they may seem.

Anyway, here are some opening lines to get the thing moving along :

'Well, what did you think?' No suggestion of negativity, just a straight question.

'How do you think that went?'

'What did you really like about that?' Positive focus – we're looking for good news stories, right?

'What were you pleased with?' Same thing.

When we continue to seek out positive responses form the coachee we start building what's called a *yes set* of positive responses; we're helping the coachee reinforce for herself just how talented and successful she already is.

We're building self-esteem, self-image, self-worth. Most people are so focused on what's wrong in their world, whether it's at work, at home, in terms of their health, their community role, or no role – they get stuck in a negative mindset. Our job is to help them sit up straight, breathe properly, hold their heads up and be proud of what they're already doing well. That's Continue & Begin: we build up a *yes set* of positivity.

We like that in Continue & Begin, because we want to build up a momentum of celebration. Why? Because when people are psychologically and emotionally strong they are much more likely to take on challenges to become *even better!*

Incidentally – well, I mean, if you really *must* know – Dmitri Uznadze discovered how helpful *yes set*s can be in stimulating repeated *habit*-ual behaviours. Check him out.

## Constructive language patterns – *nudge* comments

Ladies and gentlemen, *nudges* are so important to us. We know *tell* is a rubbish strategy to create personal change: it doesn't work – not consistently anyway.

The whole premise of Continue & Begin is to stimulate the coachee to determine for herself how she has performed against a pre-determined set of explicit standards or agreed aspirations, and to celebrate successes. And why do we celebrate successes? Yes, because we want to build ego and the confidence to perform even better. Got it? Excellent.

So, *nudges*: *nudges* work because we steer the coachee in the direction of a successful behaviour pattern we know they have performed. If we've seen them, heard them, in some way been able to experience their performance, we will have identified a performance factor which, in relation to the explicit standards or agreed aspirations, we can be confident they have delivered on. We *know* they did it well.

With *nudging*, we simply point them, in a generic way, towards the standard or aspiration.

'Tell me about [explicit standard/ambition]; how did you get on?'

'How did you go about [explicit standard/ambition]?'

'How did you get on with [x]?'

'What did you learn about that on the training course?'

'What were the things we agreed when we met last time?'

'What did you agree as a family rule on that?'

'What did you say you were going to do, from now on, with that?'

'What are the criteria for coursework presentation?'

Without telling, we can help a coachee identify the *continue to* behaviours they can usefully celebrate, and start the process of building ego. It's not just about helping people feel good though. We can *nudge* for the *begin to* behaviours as well. *Nudging* is much more effective than telling.

'Let's think about the [explicit standards/agreed aspirations]. What are they?'

'Which of the [explicit standards/agreed aspirations] might you want to reflect on?'

'How did you get on with [x]?

'Tell me about [x].'

## Constructive language patterns – challenges

Now, with support from you – the Continue & Begin fast coach – and a good set of explicit standards or agreed aspirations and some well-placed *nudges*, most individuals will identify a really good set of *begin to* behaviours to start work on. Not everyone will though – you know, it's best to be warned! Every now and again you'll come across someone who is reluctant to acknowledge any possibility they could behave in a different, maybe more productive, way.

It doesn't happen often but when it does it helps to be prepared. Maybe he feels anxious or vulnerable about acknowledging his limitations, or feels threatened by potential criticism of his performance. Or – let's be honest – there may be a blind spot in the coachee's self-perception where he considers himself to be so *awesome* he is way beyond any need for personal development: he is behaving in the most productive way already.

I've not met many people like this – it's surprisingly rare. There have been a few characters over the years though. I remember one guy in automotive; his name was Peter and he worked in Godalming in Surrey as a used-car seller. On Planet Peter he was the best of the best – Perfect Peter – except his sales figures didn't reflect that, which is a bit of a bummer. When we reviewed his performances using video mystery shopping – that's a great tool for workplace coaching by the way – at least in some sectors it is … anyway … Perfect Peter had overlooked an important factor: salespeople in his business were expected to follow a prescriptive sales process – and sell.

If you're from outside the world of commerce, a sales process is a structured conversation sales professionals use to steer a customer towards buying a product; it's pretty simple really. When it's done well a customer is fully understood and the sales pro will have found a solution just right for the customer. In Peter's case the car manufacturer *demanded* all salespeople representing their brand should follow the process – it was a requirement of employment. Except Peter didn't follow the process.

As it turned out, it was really simple to get Peter thinking through his *begin to* behaviours, despite his initial reluctance. All that was needed was to refer him to the explicit standards – in his case the sales process – and ask him which parts of the process he had delivered and which parts he'd missed.

When you focus on the reference point – the explicit standards or the agreed aspirations in family work or health work – there's no hiding place! The coaching session stops being about exploring the coachee's development needs, finding fault – remember, this can be anxiety-inducing for some folk – and it becomes a simple reference to pre-agreed standards or stated aspirations. It takes you – the coach – out of the equation and makes it purely about the coachee's performance against accepted standards. Nothing to do with you.

Here are a few useful questions you can use to help a Perfect Peter reconsider his potential for personal development – to identify and commit to a small number of *begin to* behaviours:

'Which of the [standards/aspirations] did you not deliver quite so well?'

'Which of the [standards/aspirations] did you miss out?'

'If you were [the other person/customer] what would you have thought?'

'What specifically could you have done differently?'

'So, what didn't work quite so well? Think about your [standards/aspirations].'

'If you did it again, how would you play it? Think about your [standards/aspirations].'

'What do you think you could do, to make that even better? Remember the [standards/aspirations] you committed to.'

### *Future feeling* and future orientation in time

In a moment we'll reveal the sequence of core questions we use in running a really good *New Code* Continue & Begin Fast Coaching session. First though, it's worth thinking through motivation and leverage. We talked earlier about KITAs and the difference between movement and motivation: it's really important the catalyst for behaviour change comes from within the person, not imposed from outside, otherwise *begin to* behaviours will be something the coachee feels forced to do rather than desires to do.

We know from anthropology that nature works towards definitive ends; there is a goal achievement all life forms are moving towards: reproduction, continuation of the gene pool – all that kind of stuff. We are hard-wired to achieve a series of ambitions; we have evolved *because* we are developmental organisms. Stagnation kills. Evolution sustains life.

Alfred Adler, the psychologist, identified that humans are teleological; that means we operate most effectively when we're oriented towards a goal, an objective or a specific ambition or outcome. We move towards

FUTURE FEELING . .

evolutionary goals; we *are* evolutionary. *New Code* Continue & Begin Fast Coaching recognises the influence of evolutionary goals and the positive feelings we associate with their potential achievement.

An evolutionary goal – a goal ambition – can become very real for us in our imagination. Imagination is a powerful stimulant for the release of hormones, both empowering and limiting. The sustained release of cortisol has serious debilitating effects on our minds and bodies; once released it sticks around a while too. Oxytocin makes us feel good – it doesn't last as long as cortisol though. Both can be released by the way we think, the way we imagine the world to be.

Epictetus knew a thing or two about how to think. He wrote about it in his text *The Enchiridion: The Manual of Life* in 135AD: 'What disturbs men's minds is not events but their judgements on events.'

What Epictetus knew was that we can choose what frame we put around a set of circumstances: either a positive, vibrant, optimistic and cheerful frame or a defeatist, negative, pessimistic frame. The key to happiness is to identify which form of imagined ambition we would like to consider. We harness this in *New Code* Continue & Begin.

A wise hypnotherapist friend once said to me: 'Nick, so long as we have our imaginations we can really disturb ourselves, or make ourselves feel good. Which would you prefer?' We do it all the time when we daydream. The thing is, we can *choose* what we want to daydream about.

A future ambition in Continue & Begin Fast Coaching could be an imagined video clip or an imagined sound, maybe hearing voices or music. Or we could imagine a feeling – an internal or external feeling – or we could imagine a smell or a taste. You can do that now: just think about lemon juice being squeezed into your mouth … notice how it affects you?

We can daydream a future scenario and imagine what we see, what we hear, feel, taste and smell. Then the goal ambition becomes *real* for us – our minds are masters of imagination.

A *future feeling* question asks the coachee to imagine *future feeling* and think about what, specifically, achievement will stimulate for them. Will it be a *movement-towards-pleasure* feeling or a *movement-away-from-pain* feeling?

By the way, it doesn't matter which it is – movement towards or movement away – as long as the stimulant is powerful enough to stimulate action. *Future feeling* is a fabulous way to help people transport themselves to a future time when they are performing new *begin to* behaviours with elegance and panache. When we help people access their imaginations of future performance excellence, we help them achieve a teleological inevitability.

And it's simple to do. We can help people access *future feeling* very simply, by including a carefully crafted question in our Fast Coaching question framework: 'So, as you imagine a time, soon, when you are doing this really well – elegantly, professionally, skilfully – how will you feel?' Will it be movement towards, or movement away? It doesn't matter which, as long as it creates change.

## Three chunks and seven questions

Ok, here we go!

So, we've been through the underpinning principles of Continue & Begin and we've explored some of the linguistic patterning that can help or hinder our coachee as we help her embark on her personal-change adventure.

Now it's time to take a look at the core questions in *New Code* Continue & Begin Fast Coaching. Here we go ...

In the flow chart in your workbook you'll see a small number of carefully crafted questions, sequenced in a way that is well-proven to induce strengthened ego and an enthusiasm to do even better.

The questions are 'chunked' into three areas:

1. CELEBRATE! Three questions.
2. CHANGE! Two questions.
3. COMMIT! Two questions.

Alright, so we're going to take each question, one at a time:

### Q0. Rapport

Question zero? What is he on about? Well, yes, because the rapport stuff we discussed earlier is really important. It's essential we build a friendly relationship for this brief intervention which is cheerful, positive and friendly. A wonderful man – Frank Farrelly, check him out – Frank once told me: 'Nick, you'll achieve far greater success if you have a warm heart, a smile about your lips and a twinkle in your eye!'

Frank was right.

So, before you dive in with your enthusiasm for coaching, take some time to put your coachee at ease. You can do it. Do you have any friends? Yes, I thought so. See, you already know how to be friendly. Friendly first, coaching second, ok?

### Q1. CELEBRATE!
**Self-assessment: 'So, what do you think?'**

What we want to do is to start a discussion, to open up debate around someone's performance, whether observed, reflected or recorded. Very simply we ask questions such as:

'Well, what did you think?'

'How do you think that went?'

'How've you been getting on?'

'How've you been progressing?'

'How do you feel it went?'

'How did it go for you?'

'Tell me about what just happened there?'

We're stimulating the discussion and we want the coachee to review his own behaviour and self-assess – to conduct his own measurement of his performance. Remember, we're not in the game of tell, tell, tell – that doesn't work. If we want the coachee to commit, it has to be his own assessment and his own commitment to change. Telling doesn't work, we know that now.

So where does he start? Well, we know we want to follow the Continue & Begin philosophy of building confidence and celebrating success. And we know why we do it, right? To build self-image and the capacity to take on new challenges – to stretch to new levels of attainment.

Sometimes the coachee will go straight for the *begin to* behaviours:

'I should ... (Oh no, he's a *should*-er) ... I should have written the report in font size 12. I knew it was wrong; I'm always messing it up.'

Noooo! He wants to get straight into improvement. Maybe he wants to beat himself up; we don't want that though – that's self-flagellation. We want him to feel awesomely powerful!

self-flagellation

Anyway ... fortunately, we know how to deal with the *improvement first* people, don't we? We use analogue marking. We simply move an imaginary box of *begin to* behaviours and place them over here. Where is *over here*? Anywhere away from the coachee. We want her to park those *begin to* ambitions – which are more likely to be *begin to* self-flagellations – over here, until we're ready to explore them. For now we're in the business of celebrating success and building ego. Alright?

'Ok, hey ... I'm sure there's a couple of things you might want to do differently in future, that's ok. Look, let's just park them over here for a while shall we?'

Nicely done.

Or maybe you get a non-committal response:

'It was ok I suppose. I did alright with some of it. I messed up a bit with a couple of things.'

That's fine, we can work with that. All we needed from this first question is to get the ball moving, to get into first gear. We've done that.

## Q2. CELEBRATE!
### Positive framing: 'What went well?'

So, pretty quickly we want to start building up the *continue to* behaviours – remember from earlier? The six and the three: six *continue to*'s and three *begin to*'s, or maybe it's a four and a two, or in observed behaviour, in-the-moment coaching. We might only get a two and a one – and that's fine.

So, what's the ratio? Six and three, four and two, two and one – that's right, we want the coachee to self-identify twice as many *continue to*'s as *begin to*'s – twice as many.

Now, no one at Continue & Begin secret police headquarters is going to get upset if it's a five and three, or a four and one, or a six and two – it's not a crime against the state, ok? As long as we get significantly more *continue to*'s than *begin to*'s. You know why we want plenty of *continue to* behaviours though, right? It's to build self-image. Why so few *begin to*'s though? You'll understand why specifically later on. For now, just accept it's a smart thing to do.

Alright, so we're going to get the *yes set* of *continue to*'s up and running. We can ask:

'What were you pleased with?'

'What were you happy with, in the way that went?'

'So, what went well?'

'What worked best?'

'What have you enjoyed?'

'What was good about what happened there?'

'Tell me some of the good things that went on there?'

Or something similar. We want the coachee focusing her attention on positivity, ok? So that's cool.

Maybe though, she's a bit stuck and doesn't know where to start. That's ok; we can help her. What are we measuring performance against? There has to be some reference point to compare against, some representation of excellence, or at least *good*. What have we got? Yes! We have the explicit standards or agreed aspirations. If the coachee is stuck – even if it's right at the start of the session – all we do is point them in the direction of the standards or aspirations:

'What's included in our customer service promises to customers?'

'What did you and your family agreed to about laundry?'

'What does school policy say about uniform?'

'What did you agree to include and exclude from your healthy-living diet?'

'What are the housing association rules for cooking in the communal kitchen?'

And away we go. The coachee now has a reference point for her thinking about how she has performed. We can have a conversation with her about standards or aspirations – and it's certainly not about you, the coach, and what you think. We're referring to a pre-agreed set of commitments. It's about what the coachee thinks; it's her own self-assessment.

## Q3. CELEBRATE!
**Momentum: 'What else [... were you pleased with]?'**

Once we've got the *continue to*'s on the move we'll want to really build up some momentum: let's get plenty more good things identified; let's get the coachee buzzing with confidence, maybe a confidence she hasn't felt for a long time. Maybe she's never really thought about how skilful she is or how she's already doing so many of the things she committed to in the standards or aspirations. Sometimes we forget how far we've come, don't we? *We forget to remember.*

We can build the *yes set* by encouraging the coachee to identify more and more good things she has done. Remember, whether it's an observed behaviour coaching session, reflective or recorded, there will be *continue to*'s waiting to be identified, so let's tease them out:

'What else were you pleased with?'

'What else went well?'

'How else has there been positive change?'

'Tell me some things that went well.'

'Tell me some more things that went well.'

'What other activities do you think were successful?'

'Keep going – this is great!'

'I bet there's more.'

'That's great! We can keep building this list; let's think of other ideas you think went well.'

Of course, the coachee may get stuck, she may run out of ideas. That's ok. If she gets stuck we give her a little *nudge* towards a particular behaviour or process that we know went well in the particular circumstance. *Nudging* is so cool; no telling though, ok?

So we carry on teasing good stuff out of the coachee until we've built up a good list, so she feels good and we ask her to reflect, to summarise … we ask her to summarise:

'Let's just run through that again. What are those things you did well there? Remind me.'

And we ask the coachee to self-identify that list of skills or processes or behaviours that she delivered, and by this time the coachee will be feeling good: the ego will be stronger and she'll be beginning to believe she really is accomplished, she really is doing well, she can be proud of herself. Too right, she can! Yeah!

**Coach:** You must be pleased with all those things you've done well there.

**Coachee:** Yeah I am I suppose, now I come to think about it.

**Coach:** And you can continue to do those things well, is that right?

**Coachee:** Yeah, of course I can!

**Coach:** Ok, cool.

And it's at this point we can celebrate, and we can ask the coachee to reflect on just how talented she is.

### Action planning

Now is an ideal time to make a note of these *continue to* behaviours. If you've got a Continue & Begin action plan to hand let's get the coachee to jot down the things they've said they are going to carry on doing well.

Written *continue to*'s become embedded in the mind of the coachee; we want them to realise just how talented they already are, to feel good about themselves, to have their self-worth strengthened, to feel good about themselves. Remember, people are far more likely to take on personal development ambitions if they feel resourceful and therefore confident. Let's celebrate!

Once we've maxed out on the resourcefulness we can guide the coachee towards stretch – to encourage her to do some things differently and maybe even better than she does now.

Because – when she's feeling good – we can move on to the change programme, the *begin to*'s. Her ego is strong, she feels confident, she feels empowered and capable; if she can do these things well, of course she can do other things well. Let's get on with performing to an *even better* level than this!

Now, what are these development opportunities?

## Q4. CHANGE!
### Change planning: 'What will you do differently (… or even better)?'
We can ask our coachee to celebrate her successes, to embed her feel-good and help her stand a little taller. Few of us do that enough, by the way. And then we can move on to the change piece:

'Hey, let's just think about what you might want to do a little bit differently next time round that would make your performance even better. What do you think that could be? What kind of things?'

Or we can use slightly different language patterns, each seeking the same outcome:

'What could be a good next step for you?

'What would make you feel even better next time?

'How could things improve even more?

'And what else?'

So, these are the *begin to*'s, and we only want one or two – a maximum of three *begin to*'s in the change plan. And the way we do it is to encourage the coachee to self-identify.

'What are those things that you would like to begin to do a little differently?'

Of course, they may come up with something trivial: her name badge wasn't on straight; his hair wasn't quite as smooth as he'd have liked, or whatever.

What we want is to do is make sure we've got one, two or three *begin to*'s, and we want those small number of *begin to*'s to be of a high quality and to refer back to those explicit standards and aspirations that we talked about earlier.

We may find we have to *nudge* the coachee towards something significant if they've identified trivia – hey, let's hope they've identified something juicy. If not, we go back to the standards and aspirations – every time ladies and gentlemen. It's the standards and aspirations that give us the reference points for coaching. You can't coach without a reference point.

### 'I know you don't know'

Incidentally, there's a useful *tongue fu* technique for helping people when they get stuck and can't access their unconscious mind. You can use it before or after a *nudge* – either is cool. It's called *I Know You Don't Know* and it's super-effective at unlocking mindsets. It's really great for the dunno-ers.

It goes like this:

**Coach**: So, what do you think you might want to do differently next time?

**Coachee**: I dunno.

**Coach**: Ok, think about the aspiration list you made some time ago.

**Coachee**: Yeah, I dunno.

**Coach**: Have a think.

**Coachee**: Honestly, I dunno.

**Coach**: I know you don't know, and if you did know, what would you say you might want to do differently next time?

**Coachee**: Well, I suppose I could do [x].

And away you go.

*I know you don't know* … it creates possibility by giving the coachee permission to imagine a time when they are able to know the answer to your question. I'll tell you more about this kind of thinking when we get on to the Can't to Can Belief Busting model. That will blow your mind. It's awesome!

## Q5. CHANGE!

### Implementation: 'What has to happen to make that happen?'

Implementation is important; it's vital. Remember: 'Knowing what to do …' – that's right, you know the rest of it now. Plans without implementation strategies are just wishes, just dreams. Nothing will happen unless the coachee makes a plan of implementation and then takes action!

So how can we encourage the coachee to think about implementation? Simple: we use an ace question – I call it a *freedom question* because it helps a person develop a plan of escape from their current restrictive set of circumstances. Linguists call it a modal operator of possibility or a modal operator of opportunity. A typical *freedom question* in Continue & Begin would be: 'So, what has to happen for that to happen?'

Anyway, whatever you call it – a *freedom question*, modal operator – it helps a person think about his strategy for change and, in particular, a strategy for implementation, the nuts and bolts of getting the thing done, which the coachee has identified as one of his *begin to*'s.

Here we go:

**Coach**: What has to happen for that to happen? To begin to use the new software?

**Coachee**: Well … er, I need to get on the e-learning module. I can book onto it this afternoon.

**Coach**: Ok, cool. That's a plan!

Or,

**Coach**: So, what has to happen for you to make that happen, that *begin to*, about getting up in time to make the children breakfast and get them ready for school? You said you're going to do that next Monday morning … is that right?

**Coachee**:Yeah, ok. I'll set the alarm on my phone. And put it on charge. The battery has had it.

**Coach**: Alright then, nice one. You have a plan!

What you are doing here is asking the coachee to think about next steps. A Continue & Begin plan requires action for it to become a change tool. What will the coachee do to turn the plan into an action? You may wish to vary the question a little,

'What has to happen now?'

'What will you do to make that happen?'

'What's involved now?'

'What's next to make it happen for you?'

We'd like an implementation plan wouldn't we? This is a key step in the change from *Old Code* Continue & Begin to *New Code*. Remember, a goal without an implementation plan is just a wish.

## Q6. COMMIT!

*Future feeling*: **'How will you feel?'**

So this is where the *future feeling* piece fits within fast coaching. *Future feeling* is really important for leverage.

Remember, people do things – they take action, they behave – because of feeling either an urge to move away from discomfort or pain or a move towards comfort and pleasure. We're just domesticated primates. You can read Robert Anton Wilson on that. We're just mammals who want pleasure – and no pain, thank you, apart from a few weird people and we're not going to talk about that.

So, anyway … how do we uncover a person's *future feeling* – the feeling that is most likely to make the *begin to* activities happen?

We ask them what it is!

'Let's think about some future time and place when you are doing this really well. What will that do for you? How will you feel?'

We know it's an Emotional Driver that stimulates personal behaviour changes, so what is the *future feeling* – either movement away from discomfort or movement towards pleasure? What will be the emotional benefit for the coachee?

For variety you can use:

'And what will that do for you?'

'How will you feel when you can do that really well?'

'Imagine some future time when you are really skilled at this. How will you feel?'

'What feeling of benefit will this give you?'

'And that will do what for you?'

Now we have some really cool *begin to*'s identified and the coachee has confirmed the benefits will help her feel good. Remember, it's the Emotional Driver – movement away from pain or movement towards pleasure. This is what stimulates action!

### 'Would you like that?'

This is a simple *lock in* question. It follows on naturally from the feeling question. It confirms to the coachee and the coach that the coachee will be motivated by the feeling they want to move towards, or move away from.

We need to check the strength of response here – what the NLP people call calibration. Get a firm 'Yes' and you can be confident the coachee is well on the way to making changes; get an uncertain response and you may want to check their motivation level.

### Action planning the *begin to*'s

So, earlier the coachee made a written note of her *continue to*'s on the action plan. Well, no surprise here folks, it helps if we get the *begin to*'s written down too – this is really important. Research shows that goals and plans that an individual writes down are far more likely to be actioned and achieved if they are recorded in writing. There's something about the physiological connection with cognitive processing that makes the

combo of the two super-effective – if you want your goal to be realised, write it down.

I set some goals in 2004 inspired by Brian Mayne's Goal Mapping method. Brian is a talented man; I went to school with him … ha ha!

Anyway, here's my goal map from that time. I kept it in my work briefcase for years and years. Look carefully and you'll see my timeline for achievement was 5 years. Some goals came sooner than expected, others took a little longer than I'd planned, and that's ok because without the goals being written down and in our face every day it's unlikely we will achieve something we thought about just the once.

### Q7. COMMIT!
**Commitment and follow-up: 'Is this something you're going to do?'**

Commitment

Goals – and especially written goals, and by the way, these are even more powerful when the ideas are also represented in picture form, images – have a way of stimulating our imaginations and feelings about future potential.

Of course, *future feeling* will only work if the coachee takes action. Even the best plans, even with implementation plans agreed, they are just ideas until they are implemented. The commitment mantra makes sense for most people: 'Commitment is doing the thing you said you would do, long after the mood you said it in has left you!' George Zalucki said that; go check him out. He's great value if you're into personal development. Good fun too.

Anyway we're going to finish the whole thing off by another summary:

'Remind me quickly, what are those things that you've done well? Let's run through them again. And you're going to continue to do those things well?'

'Ok, feeling good … ok … and we've identified just a couple of things you want to begin to do differently from now on. And what were they … remind me?'

It is essential we gain an unequivocal commitment from the coachee to take action, otherwise it won't happen.

So, this is the one part of Continue & Begin Fast Coaching where we become super-assertive with our eye contact. We lock on with laser vision and ask intently is this something she is *really* going to do? It's the closure piece, the acid test: is it going to happen or have we just been having a nice chat?

You'll know from your own life experiences and your intuition whether your coachee is congruent when she says she's committed to the change plan. Her *words, song and dance* will tell you if she's fully dedicated. Is she definite? Or is she a bit flimsy and uncertain?

There are plenty of commitment-seeking questions you can use at this point. What you choose will depend on your relationship with the coachee and the language patterns that are appropriate for the person's culture. You could use any of these if they fit:

'Look I just want to be clear: is this something you are going to do … are you going to do this? Are you serious about this? Is this a commitment that you're making?'

'Is this something you'll do?'

'Are you able to commit to this?'

'Are you definitely going to do this?'

'Will you do this?'

'Are you really going to do this?'

'How likely are you to do this?'

'Are you going to do this?'

'Are you committed to making this happen?'

'Are you happy to commit to this?'

'Is this something you can do on your own, or do you need help?'

'Is this doable?'

'Are you saying you're going to do this?'

'Is this a promise to yourself?'

'Do we have a contract?'

'Are you serious about this, or are you messing about!?'

An incongruent response gives you – the Continue & Begin Fast Coaching practitioner – it gives you an opportunity to explore the coachee's commitment in more detail. You might, for example, you might want to revisit the person's internal motivators. If you get a positive, congruent response that's great. Let's get on with it!

### 'Serious, or messing about?'

You know, I'm sometimes asked about this optional commitment question. It was in common use in *Old Code*. Is it really ok though, to ask, 'Are you serious or messing about?' Isn't it a bit in-yer-face? Well, there are two answers here, and both offer useful learning.

Answer number one: no, it's not necessary to use these exact words. I've already suggested a pretty expansive list of optional phrases for the coach to consider using.

Let's just reflect, the purpose of the commitment question is to create a pledge, through a personal vow, that action will be taken. This ties right back to tentative self-talk. You can use language such as:

'Are you committed to this?'
'Is this something you're going to do?'
'Will you do this?'
'Will you need help with this or will you do it on your own?'

Or any of the other commitment questions I offered earlier. In *New Code* I acknowledge this clarification.

The second answer is more interesting. Some years ago I was fortunate to spend two wonderful days with the incredible Frank Farrelly. Frank was the creator of Provocative Therapy. Now, at the time, Frank was in his mid-seventies; he was working with a small group of 12 students and I was one of them. He was cheeky and charming, and I was mesmerised by his skill and his fun approach. He was a very funny man was Frank.

During his introduction he said, 'Ok, so I'm 75. That's old. It's ok though – I'm a sex object for nonagenarians.' Provocative Therapy includes plenty of humour. Check Frank out on YouTube.

So anyway, I practised his Provocative Therapy techniques during our workshop. I was awful – completely rubbish! My *clients* were fellow students of Frank and they said I was just plain rude. Oops. Well, I had a fantastic piece of luck: I sat next to Frank at lunch one day. It was an amazing lunchtime chat. We shared our passion for motorcycling and how his wife worried about him biking at his age; we enjoyed our meal together. I felt really comfortable with him.

I told Frank how rubbish I'd been at the practical earlier that day. Then he told me his secret to provocative work: 'Nick, you need the rapport in place. You've gotta work with a smile around your lips, a twinkle in your eye and an open heart!'

Anyway, the more I practised, the more skilled I became, until I realised I had successfully modelled a few small parts of Frank's enormous repertoire. How about that! That's modelling for you. Frank died in 2013; I was so fortunate to have spent time with him.

So, in the spirit of Frank, would you like to get really good at Continue & Begin? Oh yeah? Really? Smile, twinkle, open heart? Well are you serious – or are you just messing about?

## Follow-up

Is the change plan being implemented? You'd like to know wouldn't you? This is the follow-up phase and it's really important – important for you and important for the coachee – to know you are as serious about this as they are. Sometimes people are stimulated by knowing they are being monitored.

'When shall we catch up to find out how you've done?'

'When shall we follow-up on progress?'

'When's a good time to meet up again?'

'Shall we put something in the diary to see how you're getting on?'

## Core questions summary

Alright, so let's summarise the key stages and typical questions we use in Continue & Begin Fast Coaching: the core questions ... remember the rapport first ... Question Zero, remember?

So, Question Zero – Rapport.

Question 1. CELEBRATE!
Self-Assessment: 'Well, what did you think?'

Question 2. CELEBRATE!
Positive Framing: 'What went well?'

Question 3. CELEBRATE!
Momentum: *yes set* ... 'And what else?'

Question 4. CHANGE!
Change Planning: 'What would you do differently, or maybe even better?'

Question 5. CHANGE!
Implementation: 'What has to happen, to make that happen?'

Question 6. COMMIT!
F*uture feeling*: 'How will you feel (when you are doing this really well)?'
'Would you like that?'

Question 7. COMMIT!
Commitment and follow-up: 'Is this something you will do?'

## Coachee action planning

So these are the core questions we use in Continue & Begin Fast Coaching. Let's go back to the action plan piece – there's learning to be had here.

We've got a plan, we've identified a list of *continue to*'s and just a small number of *begin to*'s – maybe it's six and three or maybe it's four and two or maybe it's a real quick Continue & Begin Fast Coaching session and it's two *continue to*'s and one *begin to*; that's cool.

Now, irrespective of the nature or the shape or the numbers involved, it's really important we get this committed on paper; Continue & Begin action plans work best when they are written down.

And whose action plan is it do you think? Yes, that's right it's the coachee's, not the coach. It's the coachee's plan, it's their celebration and it's their change plan, so they have a piece of paper, they have the pen, they do the writing. I've seen too many poor quality coaches driving on their own agenda by holding the pen, writing the plan and then giving it to the coachee – it's a camouflaged version of telling. This is the complete opposite of what this thing is about, right? We want the coachee to self-assess, to self-identify and self-commit – to *continue to* do some things really well and to *begin to* do some things differently, or maybe even better. It is *not* about the coach telling, persuading or manipulating someone to do what they are told. That's telling, and it's a crap way of trying to get someone to change.

Alright, rant over.

Now, some organisations will have a fancy learning management system where action plans can be recorded, people can access online and all this stuff; other folk are just after an old-fashioned piece of paper and it says on the top 'Continue & Begin Action Plan – *Continue To*'s and *Begin To*'s'.

Notice this though: on good action plans there's more space for the *continue to*'s than there is for the *begin to*'s, and you know why don't you? So, whatever model or method or strategy you adopt, please, please, please make sure the coachee makes a note of *their continue to*'s and makes a note of *their begin to*'s because action plans work well when they are committed to paper.

There are exceptions of course. If you're working with a coachee in a family setting, or maybe a family group, it might be difficult for the coachee or coachees to make a written note. Maybe there's literacy issues to consider or disability factors.

In such cases it makes sense to make the notes for the plan on their behalf. My guidance to you is to check – and double check – you are using their language, not your own. Remember *clean language* and the dangers of paraphrasing? Please use the coachee's language, not yours.

## Conscious competence as a Continue & Begin fast coach

Ok, enough of the detail, let's do some overview work now.

So, even the most elegant performers weren't born brilliant at their skills; they had to learn and develop until they became competent. Everyone goes through a learning process. The same applies to you in your role as a new Continue & Begin coach. It will take a little bit of time and plenty of practice for you to become a really slick operator – and that's cool. There's a learning process we go through when we embark on a new skill and we can see this described in a competency grid. There's one in your workbook.

Ok, so when we start out learning a new skill or activity we often don't know what's involved or how we are expected to operate. We don't even

CONSCIOUS INCOMPETENCE

know what a good way of operating is, or what's considered *less good*. We're ignorant. We are *unconsciously incompetent*. Pretty soon we find out there are some things we don't know how to do; we recognise we are *consciously incompetent*.

And as we learn and practise we begin to get the hang of things – if we really concentrate – and in time we become capable. Ok, we might not be super-slick to start with, but if we think about it and take our time we can do the thing we've been learning. We have to think about it though. We've become *consciously competent*.

And after a while we get so we don't need to think about how to do something – it becomes natural, we can do it easily – and we become so slick it's almost like autopilot. We've become *unconsciously competent*.

Alright, so let's think about this in the context of driving a car, in fact let's make it a hill start when you first started taking lessons. You remember that? Now then, until you started driving lessons you didn't know much about clutch control, handbrake release and all the things you need for a hill start – you were *unconsciously incompetent*. You remember though, don't you, that hill start you had to do, by the traffic lights? And there's that *significant other person* sat next to you in the passenger seat. You remember who that was.

And the lights are red, and you have one hand on the handbrake and one on the steering wheel and you're looking in your rear-view mirror. Incidentally, notice how the rear-view mirror is small ... hmmm ... it's important to look back now and again isn't it? But the windscreen is so much bigger isn't it? Hmmm ... and it's the way for forward direction as well, isn't it? Now that's something to think about.

Anyway, this is a hill start and it can be difficult, so you look in the rear-view mirror and a truck has pulled up behind you ... aargh! And the lights turn from red, to red and amber, and you press one pedal and lift up another, and you click the handbrake and ... you've stalled the engine. Oh no! Panic ... panic ... adrenaline rush ... cortisol release ... skin colouration – the car is stuck in gear and you depress the clutch. No! The car rolls backwards – no! The significant other leans across and calmly pulls up the handbrake and says, 'Ok, stay calm, take your time.'

But you're already turning the ignition key again – even though the car is still in gear – and the starter motor whizzes its disapproval, and the truck driver behind you sounds his horn, and you're getting even more anxious ... and then the lights turn red again. Oh no! This is so embarrassing.

And then eventually you get away from the lights, up the hill and away. And the more you practise, the more you move through *conscious incompetence*, through *conscious competence* – especially if you really concentrate and maybe you stick your tongue out a bit to help you concentrate – and then you get to the stage where you can do this stuff easily, almost without thinking. You've become *unconsciously competent* – like autopilot, eh?

And I wonder how many times you've driven and arrived at your destination and you've thought to yourself: 'I don't even remember driving here'. Hmmm ... that's *unconscious competence*.

Be careful though, because *unconscious competence* is what leads to bad habits that we are not consciously aware of. How many of us would pass a driving test if we had to retake it today?

My guidance to you with Continue & Begin Fast Coaching is to always keep a little conscious thought processing going during the coaching process.

## Seven plus or minus two

7 + 2 . . .

Let's do a little bit of research, a bit of studying. There was a cognitive psychologist in the 1950s called George Miller. Miller conducted research into short-term memory and our ability to consciously absorb and reproduce ideas – our thoughts and processes – from our short-term memory. What Miller identified became known as *The Magical Number Seven Plus or Minus Two*. Miller was interested in human capacity for short-term memory and the transfer of information to storage in our long-term memory.

Miller suggested short-term memory is maintained by rehearsal, by repeated application – which makes sense doesn't it – and that after a while the information is transferred to the long-term memory for what he called passive storage. He also said that if the information is not used – he called it decay or displacement – then we eventually forget the information.

Are you getting the link here with *begin to*'s in Continue & Begin Fast Coaching?

Seven plus or minus two: that means the range five to nine. Five to nine what, though? Well, a suggestion is we can – most of us anyway –

consciously juggle and hold in our short-term memory up to nine random numbers, maybe seven random words or perhaps as few as five ideas.

Now think about this – this is important for us because in the process of Continue & Begin Fast Coaching we ask the coachee to remember to implement how many *begin to*'s? That's right, a maximum – a maximum of three. My guidance to you is to make it two or one, but if you must squeeze out every last drop of value out of your coaching session never go above three.

Ok, so this fits with the research done by Miller and others like Alan Baddeley and Graham Hitch in the 1970s. Nelson Cowan in 2001 suggested short-term memory is even less capable than Miller's *Magic Number* proposals.

There is a common denominator to the research though, and that says don't be overloading people's minds with too many thing to consciously think about if you want them to recall them easily from their short-term memory.

Now, this works incredibly well when we help somebody to change the way they are operating, with just one, or maybe two, or if necessary three things to hold in the short-term memory. Don't be asking someone to be doing lots of things differently immediately; don't be encouraging them to take on masses of *begin to*'s, because frankly you're setting them up for failure.

I remember consulting for a high-profile telecoms company in the UK. I was running a training conference. We were reviewing a video featuring a sales professional helping a retail customer decide on a new cell phone. Stood next to me was the Retail Director – a big boss – he wanted results and he wanted them fast! During the video he leaned across and whispered in my ear: 'I've been counting … that guy has got 16 things wrong. He needs to start doing 16 things better immediately or he's out.'

What a cretin.

Apart from the inability of anyone to do 16 things differently immediately, the sales professional's performance said a lot about the quality of people management in that organisation. Let's explore the processes the sales guy had to follow; let's consider the calibre of training he's had; let's think about the local support he's had from his line manager. How is he being coached, or not coached? Let's measure the effectiveness of people development within that business.

Retail Director? Imbecile.

Now, whether Miller, or Cowan, or Baddeley and Hitch, or anyone else's research is accurate or not, we don't know for sure. Seven plus or minus two might be what Hans Vaihinger called – Vaihinger was a German philosopher – what Vaihinger called a *useful fiction*, that is, it doesn't really matter whether it is true or not, as long as it is useful.

In Continue & Begin Fast Coaching it is useful to limit the number of *begin to* aspirations to a modest number so the coachee doesn't have too many pieces of information to retain in his short-term memory. We encourage our coachee to identify a small number of *begin to* behaviours – things he can focus on, concentrate on, as he's going about his daily business or family life, whatever that may be.

## (Coaching) behaviour breeds behaviour

Let's think about *your* mindset, *your* state of mind during the process of Continue & Begin Fast Coaching. It's really important you're in a positive mindset and you're achievement-focused. The behaviour patterns and thought processes a coach adopts can radically improve – or jeopardise – the success of a Continue & Begin Fast Coaching session.

Now, let's just explore some of these things where behaviour breeds behaviour, and one of the things that really – you know – causes difficulties, is when folk are suffering from what I call PLOMism ... P.L.O.M. ... PLOMism: Poor-Little-Old-Me.

Now you've seen these folk I'm sure. You know, they've generally got a physiology that is a little bit pathetic, and they're not focused on success, and there is a lot of sighing going on. Everybody gets a little bit of PLOM from time to time, except in your role as a Continue & Begin coach it's critical you stay upbeat and positive and solution-focused – that you're full of energy and positivity about achievement.

If you're suffering from PLOMism, guess what? You're coachee is going to start suffering from it very soon – yeah, it's contagious – and

PLOM

it's absolutely essential we move out any PLOMism from the environment for coaching, because it's critical we're achievement-minded and we're thinking about goals. We don't want to infect our coachee, do we?

Let's think of some other debilitating, un-resourceful mindsets – some other behaviours that get in the way. What about the person who's what I call an *R-But*-er. An 'Ah!' and a 'But'. These are the folk that, when you've got a bright new idea, they say, 'Ah, but I'll tell you why that won't work'.

R-BUT

It's the negative mindset we can't afford to have there in the process of Continue & Begin Fast Coaching. We have to be focused on positivity, on goal achievement, otherwise the whole thing just crumbles; it falls apart like a pack of cards.

Closely related to the *R-But* are the *CAVE* people.

CAVE

You know, every now and again you might meet a cave dweller: C-A-V-E, those people who are Continually Against Virtually Everything. Have you met them? They are closely related to the *R-Buts*; they hang out together in caves; you know, misery loves company, doesn't it. It's not helpful if we want people to celebrate things they're doing well and to strive for further achievement, new ideas, new ambitions. CAVE people inhibit that kind of thinking.

What about the *ICBA*'s? I-C-B-A ... I – Can't – Be ... Bothered.

ICBA

If you're not full of dynamism and energy as we set about Continue & Begin Fast Coaching plans for your team members, or your colleagues, or your friend, or your family members, or whoever it is that you're helping, if you're not full of that dynamism – guess what? They're not going to be full of it either. It's contagious, *ICBA*'s.

Then there's the *Mood Hoovers*!

MOOD HOOVER

Oh my word, these are the people that come in the room and it's like they have a massive industrial-sized vacuum cleaner, and they suck energy and positivity from the room – and you can see people being deflated. In fact, as they walk in the room, you can see the folks spot them as they're walking in and they say, 'Oh no, here she is …'. These people are not helping, they're not providing an environment of positivity and challenge and adventure.

*Mood Vampires* are closely related to *Mood Hoovers*, and are just as bad. These are the people who sink their fangs into your neck – you know, as vampires spread their 'love', well they infect people; they sink their fangs in and they fill them full of negativity – and then they become vampires too. And the classic one: you know, you hear people who whinge and whine, and as they whinge and whine they sink their fangs into everybody else and encourage them to think how bad everything is – and it's very easy to get sucked into that. We can't afford to be operating as a *Mood Vampire* in your role as a coach.

How about the *MGs* – Moaners and Groaners?

MG

Have you spotted any of those? They usually come in twos: one moans while the other one groans. The first one moans and the second one says, 'It's worse than that, let me tell you.' And the moaners say, 'I didn't know it was that bad.' And they disappear into a vortex of negativity.

The Moaners and the Groaners – the *MGs* – no place for it at Continue & Begin. So debilitating.

There is one other category I'd like to bring to your attention: it's the 20-20s. In most environments – whether it's work or social or sporting, or whatever – it may be there's somebody who's been there, seen it and done it … and you can't teach them anything, can you?

They've got 20 years' experience. Well, I'm going to tell you they haven't got 20 years' experience at all; they've got one year's experience that's been repeated every year, in the same way, irrespective of the world changing around them. They haven't got 20 years' experience – they've got one year's experience multiplied 20 times. You understand the difference?

20/20

That's why new people – young people especially – are so dynamic, because they don't know what the rules are, and the embedded thought patterns, the restricted thinking habits; they think in new ways and sometimes they come up with something amazing. So 20:20s have a choice: evolve or get left behind. You can't be a 20:20 with Continue & Begin and then expect your coachee to be innovative – to explore opportunities and future possibilities. Human evolution is built on new, habit-breaking behaviours.

To grow and develop we will benefit from being open minded, and Continue & Begin Fast Coaching is new and it's innovative, and it's evolving and changing like *New Code*. And for many of the people you introduce it to it'll be the first time they've experienced anything like it. Use it with passion and energy – and that will infect. Let's infect people with passion; let's infect them with innovation and excitement.

Now we can start to develop people's change plans, which are built on positivity rather than all these negative mindsets. Your behaviour as a Continue & Begin coach will stimulate reflected behaviour in your coachee.

## Can't to Can Belief Busting

So, earlier I talked about the world's worst question: remember what that is? Yeah, '**Why can't you**? **Why can't you** do that thing? How many times have I told you? I've told you, and I've told you … **why can't you** do it?'

It's a dreadful question to ask, and the reason why it's so dreadful is … remember the assertive question technique? When you ask somebody assertively they go on a journey to answer that question. When you ask somebody, 'Why can't you do it?' they go on the journey; they search through the filing cabinets of their mind until they find the word document with all of the reasons why they can't do it.

They *believe* that they can't do it; they make a *decision* they can't do it and they make a list to confirm all those reasons why they can't do it. It's important to make a list if you're going to justify yourself, right?

Then they present you with the list, and they reinforce their belief system and the decision they made because they want to be certain – and you wouldn't want to be uncertain about not being able to do something

would you? And they have a really impressive list of excuses and justifications: 'These are all the reasons why I can't do that thing. Thank you for asking.'

What happens when you ask somebody 'Why can't you ...' do something is – it just cements in their mind the decision they've made that they can't.

Well now, I've got to tell you, many years ago I had managers coming to see me who were very bright, articulate, eloquent communicators, intelligent people. Once we started to spend time together it was apparent that *even though* they were sophisticated communicators and confident – at least in their presenting style – beneath the veneer of confidence were all sorts of gremlins and things going on in their mind, with that critical inner voice telling them that they can't do certain things.

Common ones were things like: 'I can't do presentations.' 'I can't deal with conflict.' 'I can't sell.' 'I can't write reports.' 'I can't speak at conference.' 'I can't be assertive with my boss.'

Can't ...

Well, it's not true. Of course it's not true, but what people sometimes do is they create for themselves a tissue-paper prison. It's not a real prison at all; they can break out and step outside anytime they like, but they prefer to live inside their imaginary limiting beliefs – a tissue-paper prison. They've made a decision: 'I can't do that, it's not me, I'm not that kind of person. Don't ask me to do it any more '

Well, what do we do under those circumstances? We could ask the rubbish question 'Why can't you do it?' and we know what happens then, don't we? No, much better, I developed something called Can't to Can Belief Busting, which is the most powerful framework for creating change you're ever going to come across.

This is a tool for you and it's wonderful. You can use it at work, you can use it in a community environment, can use it at home, you can use it with yourself and it's very, very powerful. What we do is we take the framework – the flow chart of Can't to Can, you can see it in your workbooks … that's right – and we start at the bottom and work our way up to a position of freedom and opportunity.

We start at the bottom with a tissue-paper prison and we identify what is the limiting belief, what is the decision someone's made about their inability to do something, and we identify that, but instead of asking *why* they can't do it we turn it round and we say:

**Coach**: Ok, I understand what you've said. Tell me, what would happen if you could do that thing?

What would happen
if you could … ?

159

**Coachee**: But I can't.

**Coach**: I know you say you can't. Just bear with me, imagine – just pretend – what will happen if you are able to do it? Imagine some future time and place where you can do it; in fact you're really good at it. Just imagine.

Sometimes people get really stuck: 'I don't know ...' Stuck. And we can help them with that great question ... remember?

**Coach**: I know you don't know, and if you did know, what would happen if you were able to do it really well? Just imagine.

**Coachee**: Well, it would be good obviously.

And what happens is something quite remarkable ... because ... what we're looking for here is benefits ... some form of emotional leverage ... so we can follow-up and ask the question:

**Coach**: So, how will you be feeling when you're doing that thing really well? Imagine you're doing it now, and you're really good at it. What feelings will you have?

**Coachee**: It would be great. I don't know ... I'd be proud I suppose. I'd feel good. I'd feel happy.

**Coach**: Well would you like that? That feeling of pride, that feel-good ... feeling happy? Would you like those things? Being able to do that thing you thought you couldn't.

**Coachee**: Well, yeah, of course I'd like that.

**Coach**: Well alright then!

Because now what's happened is we've done the most difficult thing: we've got them to consider – just *consider* – the possibility that they may be able to do that thing, maybe not now but sometime in the future when they are more resourceful. That was the tricky bit.

Now all we have to do is map out how they're going to do it, and the way we do that is by repeating the same question – I call it the *freedom question* – and you keep repeating it time after time. My question is this – and you might want to phrase this a little differently each time – and the question is this: 'What would have to happen to make that happen?'

And we keep asking it: 'What has to happen to make that happen?' And maybe we might phrase it a bit differently: 'And how can you make that happen?' And keep asking it:'Ok, and what has to happen to make that happen?' and keep asking, until we get to the first move – the first step in maybe a sizeable journey, the first piece of behaviour that's going to help the individual move towards freedom and opportunity. We keep asking it and then – when we get the first step identified – it's at that point that we summarise and we'll say:

**Coach**: Well, let me just see if I've got this right: what you're going to do is ... and you're going to do it like this ... and a result of doing it like this ... you're going to be able to do that thing ... which you believed that you couldn't. Is that right?

**Coachee**: Yes.

And at the top of the flow chart you'll see *Time Specific* and we'll ask her:

**Coach**: So, when are you going to take that first step, that first action?

**Coachee**: Soon.

What! Don't give me 'soon'. We don't want soon. We want specificity!

**Coach**: Ok, cool. When specifically are you going to do that?

And we include a *convincer*. It's important we help the coachee remind herself of the emotional benefit – the feeling benefit – of making this happen. This is crucial. It's the feeling she will access that will stimulate her into action, the movement away or movement towards that she craves.

**Coach**: Ok, and remind me – what will that do for you? What feelings will you have, when you're able to do that thing?

**Coachee**: You know – proud, happy. I'd feel good about it.

**Coach**: And you'd like that would you?

**Coachee**: Well, of course I would!

**Coach**: Well, there we are then! Fantastic, all we need to decide now is when you're going to do it.

And we close the whole thing off by asking them to commit, with questions like:

'Is this something you're going to do?'
'Do you need any help to do this, or can you do it on your own?'
'Are you serious about this?'
'Are you committed to this plan?'
'Is this a promise to yourself?'

And it's the one part of the process where we have super-assertive eye contact. It's really important the coachee makes a pledge to herself and, by implication, it's a pledge to you as well. Some people are driven more by pleasing others than they are by pleasing themselves – it's a fact.

And you might want to agree a follow-up call, or a meeting or something, to check on progress. This tends to stimulate action because the coachee knows you're expecting action, not just words. And that's what we want isn't it? We want *do*, not *know*.

Once we've got an affirmation from them and we have a Can't to Can action plan in place, it's very, very powerful.

So, ladies and gentlemen, I'm giving this to you – it's my gift. It's a wonderful thing to use it and spread the word because Can't to Can helps people feel wonderful; it can help them do the thing ... the thing they didn't realise they had the potential to do.

At the heart of Can't to Can are those fab *freedom questions*:

'What would happen if you could?'

'What would have to happen to make that happen?'

There's a fancy phrase for these questions: they're called Modal Operators of Possibility. You can read about that if you like.

And remember the 'I know you don't know ...' question, of course, only if you need it; that's a very cool tool: 'I know you don't know, and if you did know, what would you say the answer is?'

So, the Can't to Can Belief Busting flowchart is in your workbook. Remember, we start from the bottom with the limiting belief – the tissue-paper prison – and then you're on the way up.

## Can't to Can Belief Busting flow chart

**Action!**

### Commitment

- Is this something you'll do?
- Are you committed to making this happen?
- Is this do-able?
- Is this a promise to yourself?

- Can you do this on your own or do you need help?
- Are you happy to commit to this?
- Are you saying you're going to do this?
- Are you serious or just messing about?

### Emotional Driver Check

And remind me …
What will that do for you?
How will it make you feel?

### Confirmation of Emotional Driver

And you'd like that?

### Summarise

Let me see if I've got this right …

### Summary confirmation

Is that correct?

### Time specification

When will you do this (specifically)?

### *Freedom question* 2

What would have to happen (to make that happen)?

### Repeats

What would have to happen (to make *that* happen)?

How could you do *that*?
What options do you have?
What would be a first step?

### Emotional Driver

So, what feelings will you have … *when* you are able to do that, really well?

### Confirmation of Emotional Driver

And would you like that?

### Freedom Thinking

Imagine a future time and space when you can (do that thing) really well …
Bear with me … What would that do for you? How would you benefit from that?
How would it make you feel? Just imagine it … Just pretend … If you could …

**Limiting belief**
**Tissue-paper prison**
**'I can't (do that thing)'**

### *Freedom question* 1

What would happen if you could?

Now, before you dive in and start Can't to Can-ing everybody you meet, there's a few parameters it's worth knowing about, a few restricting factors.

Ok, so here's the first restricting factor: we know Can't to Can is amazing and it works really well if the coachee wants to do the thing they currently believe they can't. It doesn't work if the individual doesn't want to break free of their limiting beliefs. Remember it's *Can't to Can*, not *Won't to Will* – right?

Sometimes – in fact often – there's what's called a secondary gain from their limiting belief. Secondary gains are things like avoiding having to feel uncomfortable, not having to feel vulnerable, being certain. Or the flipside: avoiding feeling uncertain – notice how these secondary gains relate to *feeling*, because that's what drives behaviour, remember, movement away from discomfort or movement towards pleasure.

Ok, second limiting factor is it has to be sensible. I remember one idiot in a seminar I was running and he said: 'Well, I don't believe I can jump off a high-rise building and fly like a bird – but I'd like to fly. Does Can't to Can work for that?'

Dullard. Some people are just seeking significance. So I said, 'Well, you never know, I think you should give it a go and see what happens.'

Third restricting factor is we can only address one line of enquiry at a time. So ... someone says, 'I'd like to play golf with my work colleagues but I can't do it. I've never played and I wouldn't be able to compete with them. It would be embarrassing.'

So, we have a few lines of enquiry to explore here: lessons are probably in the mix, finding a golf club of course, hiring or buying some golf equipment – what are they called, golf bats or something – I can't stand golf. I know it's important to some people. Anyway, maybe time is a factor as well – your coachee will want to find time to play. And money of course, they'll need cash to pay for the clubs, golf bag, lessons etc. and all those awful clothes you have to wear, apparently.

So there's a few things to explore to get from 'Can't' to 'Can'. We can only explore one line of enquiry at a time, so maybe with this example we could start with ... I don't know ... finding time? The best way of selecting the starting point, of course, is to ask the coachee. Chances are, the biggest hurdle will be the one he or she raises first, that's what usually happens. Then we work through each limiter one at a time. Sometimes there's only one factor and then that's easy, and instead of being *fast* coaching, it's *super-fast* coaching.

So, there we have it: Can'to Can Belief Busting. It's an awesome tool for helping people escape from their own tissue-paper prisons. It's just a decision they made some time ago. They can make a new decision.

Like you, you can make a decision – a decision to use Can't to Can Belief Busting. Like the seven Questions in Continue & Begin Fast Coaching, it only works if you practise it and use it.

## Narrow and deep, shallow and wide

Ok ... so we've been helping an individual create changes in his or her life, that's cool – what a wonderful thing to do. Here's the next thing though, we're creating change in one person. Imagine what would happen if we could stimulate change in lots of people.

When we help an individual with Continue & Begin Fast Coaching we coach in a format I call *narrow and deep*: that means we work with just one person and we help them develop an action plan which is rich in *continue to*'s, and has a few well thought through *begin to*'s. Maybe we build a six and three, or a four and two, or maybe it's a quick two and one. That's cool; whatever we've done to help them has evolved into a celebration and a commitment to grow in that one person.

If the coachee is part of a larger living unit – a family, a workplace team, an education centre, a sports team or whatever – we can amplify the effect of the Continue & Begin action plan by working *shallow and wide*. What do I mean by that?

Well, we can run a group, or family, or class, or team coaching session: we can call it a *one-to-many* event.

*Nudge* sessions work really well when the other people within the group are likely to have the same ambitions as the primary coachee, the person who has been through a *narrow and deep* Continue & Begin session.

Where the other members share similar explicit standards or aspirations as the main coachee, they will almost certainly be interested in what the

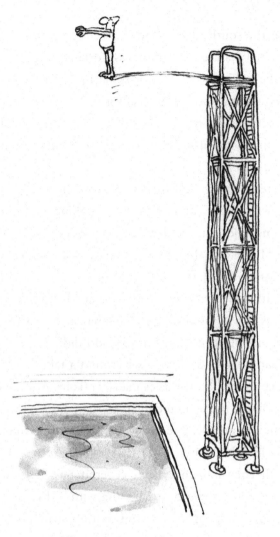

**NARROW AND DEEP**

coachee has excelled at and which *begin to*'s she has committed to work on, after all, the other members of the team have common goals. Let me give you an example: this is from a commercial environment and, like the *patterns which connect*, the principle can be applied in all sorts of different contexts.

### *One-to-many* Continue & Begin Fast Coaching

So, way back in the nineties I was working for a UK Government-funded agency as a business consultant for SMEs. My patch was Hampshire and

Dorset, in the south of England. I received a call from the owner of an environmental management business working in the oil industry. I'd been advising the business owners for some time. The owner was a dynamic guy, full of energy and ready to absorb new ideas, we'll call him Peter – because that was his name. He called me and said, 'Hi Nick, it's Peter here, I'm following up from the coaching event you ran for the business a few weeks ago.'

'Hi Peter, great to hear from you. How's it going?'

'Well, we've been running the fast coaching with our customer service and inbound sales guys and we've been doing some innovating; there's something I'd like to show you. I think you'll be interested. It's a kind of next-step thing for sharing with the whole team,' he said. 'I wondered if you'd like to come over and have a look at what we've been up to?'

Well yes, I was interested – very interested – so I went over and met with Peter and his team, and I'm so glad I did!

Pete had his inbound team sat around a table and he introduced me to everyone, including the sales manager Toby. Toby started the meeting and asked one of the team members to share his Continue & Begin action plan. I can't remember the sales exec's name – I think it was Kirsty or something like that. Anyway, Kirsty spoke about her recent fast coaching session with Toby and what they'd covered. She was describing a reflective coaching session – she'd been chatting with Toby about how she'd been following the company's sales conversation structure, and the processes and admin stuff.

It was all about a particular product category – something to do with oil reclamation equipment – and the company had a specific process for inbound sales staff to follow.

So this is how it went: Toby says, 'Ok everybody, thanks for coming. Kirsty is going to take us through her coaching action plan, and I'd like you to think about your performance in the sales areas she's going to describe: what are you good at and what are you less good at.'

Good man ... he'd been paying attention at the Continue & Begin Fast Coaching day!

So Kirsty told us all about her fast coaching session with Toby. She told us about her *continue to*'s – there were four of those – and I remember how, the more she reflected on what she'd done well, the more she sat up straighter and she told everyone about how chuffed she was with what she'd done well.

Kirsty's colleagues were paying attention and taking notes, and then she started on her *begin to*'s. I can't remember what they were except they were something to do with following the steps in the company's sales process and how she was determined to include these missing parts from now, you know, with inbound calls from potential customers. She had two of them – two *begin to*'s

I was impressed. When she'd finished, Toby – the sales manager guy – he says to the rest of the team: 'Ok everyone … so, thanks Kirsty. Now, what have you the rest of you got? What are your twos and ones?'

I was intrigued; what was going on here? Well, what the guy was doing – Toby, the sales manager – he was asking the rest of the team to think about what they'd heard from Kirsty and to reflect on their own performance in this area of their sales function. How do they perform in those circumstances, in that situation, with that kind of enquiry, within that product category?

Well anyway, the sales guys began to share their two and one plans with their colleagues: two things they were already doing really well in this area – this sort of enquiry – and just one key area they wanted to *begin to* do differently and maybe even better.

It was powerful stuff. I realised what Peter and Toby had done: they'd taken the *narrow and deep* individual change plan from Kirsty and amplified its impact by using it as a catalyst to create wider change amongst the team. They'd created a *shallow and wide* set of change plans – for the whole sales team! Everyone was involved and had grown as a result of one person's Continue & Begin action plan. How about that!

I realised this was an important development. I began to refer to this approach as a *one-to-many* coaching session. There was a pattern which connects; I knew this was something that could be transferred to other environments.

SHALLOW AND WIDE

A few years later I had a similar experience in a car dealership. I was asked to attend their sales meeting one evening after business. They had a parallel approach to the environmental business, only with a bit of a twist. Auto dealerships, they're kind of franchises. Anyway, they are usually required by their manufacturer to get involved in a video mystery shopping programme – you know, hidden cameras, secret shoppers and all that; it's really common in automotive.

So this dealership was no different and I showed up to their sales meeting. The dealer principal – the owner really – anyway he introduced me and I sat through almost exactly the same format, only this time using mystery shop films as the reference point. It was really powerful!

Shallow and wide!

## Developments in *one-to-many* Continue & Begin

Over the years there have been further developments in the one-to-many approach. Some organisations include their whole team in performance assessments – a kind of peer group approach, a bit like a 360-degree appraisal. There has to be massive trust and careful use of language for this to work effectively. The supportive language patterns in Continue & Begin become even more important in this context, so training in Continue & Begin is essential for this to work well. When it does work well, it has an impressive, positive impact on culture, and on behaviours.

Other organisations have what they call in-the-moment peer group coaching sessions. This is really cool: colleagues, team members, or other people in the group – with prior agreement from the coachee – they agree to offer a fast coaching session to the individual immediately after she has 'performed', whether that's a sports performance, an arts or social event, a work activity or in an educational context – even in a therapeutic environment.

## Whole team begin to

Ok, so a development of the *one-to-many* approach is the *whole team begin to*. When the *one-to-many* is complete, smart leaders, managers or influencers can suggest a collective, single *begin to* for the group to commit to. This works really well when it's presented in a campaign style – maybe a commitment made by the group – whether that's a work group, sports team, education class, family unit or some other collective of common-interest people.

On the back of a *one-to-one* and subsequent *one-to-many* fast coaching session, a sports team may make a *whole team begin to* commitment to, say, all squad players be at training on Thursday night next week – as well as the usual Tuesday – because it's a big cup match on Saturday. Get it? Everyone in.

Maybe a family unit will make a *whole team begin to* commitment to make their own beds while Mum or Dad are away on business, or do their own laundry, or agree to each member of the family cooking one shared meal each week. Or a work team – on the back of *one-to-one* and *one-to-many* coaching sessions – they might collectively agree that during December they will all work an extra 30 minutes each day to cope with seasonal workload. Or a performing arts class will agree to make their own costumes for the next musical.

### A reminder on follow-up

Alright, let's remember follow-up. So, you've got an action plan from your coaching session … nice work. It's not enough though.

Remember – knowing what to do is not the same as doing what you know. A plan is just hot air, it's just words; it means nothing until it's turned into behaviour. So the question is: has it been implemented? Is it being done? Have all those fine ambitions been fulfilled – or at least are they underway?

A carefully constructed Continue & Begin Fast Coaching action plan or Can't to Can plan deserves a professional follow-up. Your follow-up will measure progress against plan, and it might result in revisions to the coachee's original personal strategy. Follow-up requires a firm commitment from both you and the person you are helping.

So, when specifically, will you and your coachee revisit her action plan? Will you do it by phone? In person? By Skype? Facetime?

### Tentative language and tentative offenders

Tentative

Now, this is important: the language people use is a window to the soul. We can understand the likelihood of a coachee taking action on his Continue & Begin plan by the language he uses.

If you're a smart operator you'll be listening to the words the coachee uses and the tonality with which he uses them. Most people don't listen carefully – not with enough sensory acuity anyway – to recognise the emotion behind the speaker's words. We hear the sound coming from a communicator and it washes over us like a wave of noise. This is different to the utterance stuff we explored earlier – you know *deletion, distortion, generalisation* and all that. Here I'm suggesting you might want to listen to the coachee's words and any clues they may present about determination and intent.

Tentative language is a clear indicator of tentative ambition. Uncertain words, phrases and tonality give the game away and act as warning signs to the Continue & Begin fast coach.

The word *try* is a prime example of language used by a *tentative offender*. When someone tries to do something they are acting in a half-hearted, non-committed way. Chances are they are not going to deliver the goods.

Really? How can we be so confident that *try* will lead to non-delivery? It's all to do with mindset.

Remember that stuff about the unconscious mind? You know, the autonomic nervous system and all that? Our unconscious minds are super-powerful at dealing with survival management – breathing, heart pumping, body temperature control and instinct awareness, that kind of thing. It keeps us alive. Beyond that, though, it's bone idle. It will commit to nothing extra unless it absolutely has to. I don't know ... maybe it needs a rest after all that survival management activity.

Anyway, when we give ourselves a tentative instruction the unconscious mind gets into ICBA mode – It Can't Be Arsed. It behaves like a stroppy teenager; you can almost hear it saying, 'Yeah, whatever ...' Tentative language is going to achieve very little, folks.

So, what kind of language do I mean by tentative? Here are a few examples I've heard over the years when it comes to coachee commitment to action:

'I'll try ...'
'I'll do my best ...'
'I'll give it a go ...'
'It should be ok ...'

'I might be able to ...'
'I suppose ...'
'Hopefully ...'
'Yeah ... [pause]'

The above patterns are often followed by a trailing voice – the sentence dropping we talked about in the But Monster. In fact, any sentence dropping is an indication of tentativity – I'm not sure that's a word ... well, it is now.

So why does this happen? We know from therapeutic practices that our minds respond to firm assertive instructions, like the presupposition stuff we explored in 'What else ...?' and 'Anything else ...?' We respond more immediately to firmness than we do to weak, tentative requests.

This applies equally to internal dialogue or self-talk. Imagine a drill sergeant – you know, a Sergeant Major kind of character – imagine him (it's usually a him) imagine him coming out onto the parade square and he says [NDK has quiet, hesitant voice, legs crossed, avoiding eye contact, looking down at hands, picking at fingernails]: 'Er, I wondered if ... er ... I don't know ... er ... I wondered if maybe ... you know ... er... if you might like to ... er ... do a bit of marching ... er... what do you think?'

No! Of course he doesn't! He comes onto the parade group and shouts [NDK adopts pose of drill sergeant, leaning forward, chin extended, scowling, imaginary pace stick under his arm]: 'Right you 'orrible lot! I'm your mother now! Atten ... shun!'

And all the squaddies jump to attention and do exactly they're told. That's your unconscious mind for you. Give it firm instructions and it does what it's told. You don't have to shout at it, just be firm. Be tentative though, and you've got a lazy teenager on your hands ... 'Yeah, whatever ...'

Listen out for the language your coachee uses during the commitment phase. What's her commitment language like? Strong words with tonality and physiology to back it up? Firm and definite? Or uncertain and tentative, with tone and body language suggesting she's not truly committed?

This applies to both Continue & Begin core questions and Can't to Can Belief Busting.

# PART 3

*new code
continue &
begin – the
question sets*

Part 3 presents a simple flow through the core question steps in *New Code* Continue & Begin Fast Coaching and Can't to Can Belief Busting. If you want to skip straight to the framework of questions, this is the section for you. It's concise, targeted and presents the core questions used in these fast-acting approaches to people change.

Please note though, true professionalism comes from a deep underpinning knowledge and understanding, not simply rote learning and replicating a set of questions.

It's great to use Continue & Begin as a structured question set; it's even more rewarding when you understand how it works. Part 1 and Part 2 lead the reader towards a heightened awareness and a deeper understanding of how to facilitate Fast Coaching or Can't to Can Belief Busting with elegance.

If you haven't already done so, take time out to explore and discover new learning in the earlier parts of this book.

## *New Code* Continue & Begin Fast Coaching: 3 Chunks, 7 Questions

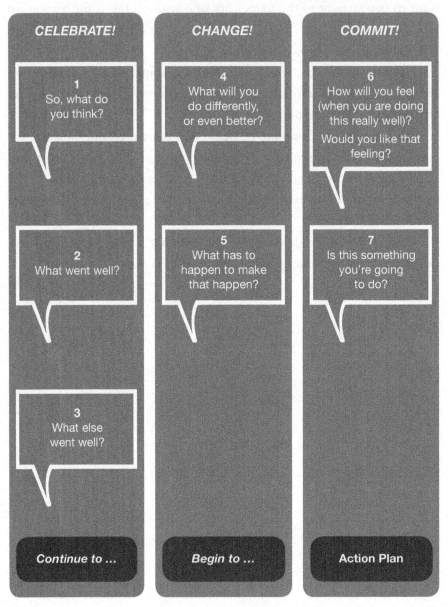

**CELEBRATE!**

**1** So, what do you think?

**2** What went well?

**3** What else went well?

Continue to ...

**CHANGE!**

**4** What will you do differently, or even better?

**5** What has to happen to make that happen?

Begin to ...

**COMMIT!**

**6** How will you feel (when you are doing this really well)? Would you like that feeling?

**7** Is this something you're going to do?

Action Plan

# Pattern Variations – CELEBRATE!

**CELEBRATE!**

**1**
So, what do
you think?
(Self-assessment)

Variations
- How do you think
  that went?
- How have you been
  getting on?
- How's it gone?
- What's been
  happening?
- What's your
  assessment?

**2**
What went well?
(Positive framing)

Variations
- What were you
  pleased with?
- What was good?
- What did you like?
- What have you
  enjoyed?
- What worked best?

**3**
What else went well?
(Momentum *yes set*)

Variations
- Tell me some other
  things you were
  pleased with.
- In what other ways
  have you done well?
- And how else has
  there been change?

*Continue to ...*

# Pattern Variations – CHANGE!

**CHANGE!**

## 4
### What would you do differently, or maybe even better?
### (Change planning)

- What changes would you make to the way you did that?
- What could be the next step?
- What would make you feel even better?
- How could things improve even more?
- If you had to do it again, how would play it?
- How do you think X was thinking and feeling?
- If you were X what would you be feeling?
- What do you think you could do differently next time?
- So, what worked less well?
- I know you don't know, and if you did know, what would you do differently?
- What specifically could you have done?
- And what else?

## 5
### What has to happen, to make that happen?
### (Implementation)

- What has to happen now?
- What will you do to make that happen?
- What's involved now?
- What's next to make it happen for you?
- How can you do that?
- How can you make that happen?

**Begin to ...**

# Pattern Variations – COMMIT!

**COMMIT!**

## 6
How will you feel (when you are doing this really well)?
*Future feeling*

- And what will that do for you?
- Imagine some future time and place when you are really good/skilled/accomplished at this. How will you feel?
- What feeling benefit will this give you?
- And that will do what for you?
- What's going on for you when you're doing that really well?
- Nice feeling?
- Feel good?
- Would you like that?
- Would you like that feeling?

## 7
Is this something you're going to do?
*Commitment & follow-up*

- Are you going to do this?
- Are you committed to making this happen?
- Are you happy to commit to this?
- Is this something you can do on your own, or do you need help?
- Are you serious about making this happen or was this just a nice chat?
- Is this do-able?
- Are you saying you're going to do this?
- Is this a promise to yourself?
- Are you serious or just messing about?
- When shall we catch up to find out how you've done?
- When shall we follow-up on progress?

**Action Plan**

# Language Checklist

| GOOD | LESS GOOD |
|---|---|
| Coaching style | Training, mentoring, counselling, KITAs |
| Ask | Tell |
| Seeking specificity | Accepting ambiguity – *deletion, distortion, generalisation* |
| Discover coachee's *deep structure* and meaning | Accepting *surface structure* utterances |
| Observation comments to stimulate conversation | Comments that pass judgement, opinion, mind-reading, verdict |
| Exploring the coachee's Structure of Well-Done-Ness | Giving *chocolate praise* |
| Opening lines<br>*Nudges*<br>Challenges | But Monsters, *should*-ing, *must*-ing, need to, have to, got to, ought to (and other language that hurts) |
| Use Continue & Begin core questions | Going off-piste |
| What else? (presupposition) | Anything else?(tentative) |
| Continue & Begin 2:1 ratio<br>3 or less *begin to*'s | Wrong ratio<br>Too many *begin to*'s |
| *Freedom questions*<br>Modal operators of possibility | Failing to use |
| *Future feeling* questions | Failing to use |
| Implementation plan questions | Failing to use |
| Commitment questions and follow-up<br>Check for tentative commitment | Failing to use |

# *New Code* Can't to Can Belief Busting

**Action!**

| **Emotional Driver Check** | **Confirmation of Emotional Driver** |
|---|---|
| And remind me ... What will that do for you? How will it make you feel? | And you'd like that? |

| **Summarise** | **Summary confirmation** |
|---|---|
| Let me see if I've got this right ... | Is that correct? |

**Time specification**

When will you do this (specifically)?

| *Freedom question* 2 | **Repeats** | How could you do *that*? |
|---|---|---|
| What would have to happen (to make that happen)? | What would have to happen (to make *that* happen)? | What options do you have? What would be a first step? |

| **Emotional Driver** | **Confirmation of Emotional Driver** |
|---|---|
| So, what feelings will you have ... *when* you are able to do that, really well? | And would you like that? |

**Freedom Thinking**

Imagine a future time and space when you can (do that thing) really well ...
Bear with me ... What would that do for you? How would you benefit from that?
How would it make you feel? Just imagine it ... Just pretend ... If you could ...

**Limiting belief**
**Tissue-paper prison**
**'I can't (do that thing)'**

| | *Freedom question* 1 |
|---|---|
| | What would happen if you could? |

# PART 4

coaching
session
transcripts

Part 4 presents a series of transcripts from coaching sessions. Included in the presentations are:

## *New Code* Continue & Begin Fast Coaching

1. Parenting: school attendance, early stage intervention;
2. Sport: teenage rugby players' skills development;
3. Call centre: inbound customer enquiries (telecoms);
4. Big ticket retail: understanding the customer;
5. Family coaching: helping Mum and going to school.

## *New Code* Can't to Can Belief Busting

1. Healthcare: time and personal management;
2. Housing support: breaking through beliefs about gaining work;
3. High street retail: managing price differentials;
4. Automotive aftersales: service care plans;
5. Call centre: solving technical difficulties for customers.

Examples are provided from commercial enterprises and community environments. While it is clearly impossible to present a comprehensive range of scenarios, these transcripts provide the reader with a sufficient range of applications to enable an understanding of the *patterns which connect.*

# *New Code* Continue & Begin Fast Coaching

## Example 1: Parenting – school attendance, early stage intervention

*Working Together to Safeguard Children* is a UK Government guide (Department for Education) to inter-agency working. The document supports professionals to safeguard and promote the welfare of children and offers guidance to agency professionals on adopting a co-ordinated approach to child protection.

As part of a multi-agency team supporting Family M children (Ryan age 11 and Christie-Lee age 7) the family worker case holder has communicated with school and discussed Ryan and Christie-Lee's attendance. This coaching session aims to support and develop the parenting skills of Ryan and Christie-Lee's mother, Jenny M.

The first part of the conversation, steered by the family worker, is about gaining clarity and agreement on the aspirations of the parent (Jenny), her ambitions for routine and a set of rules within her family (Family M) to help improve the school attendance of her two children.

Continue & Begin Fast Coaching works most effectively when a set of reference points is available for the coachee to consider.

**Family Worker**: Ok Jenny, so how's it been going since the last time we met?

**Jenny**: Like what?

**FW**: How've you been getting on with Ryan and Christie-Lee and their school attendance?

**J**: Ok.

**FW**: Alright … so, in what way has it been 'ok'? What's gone well?

**J**: What do you mean?

**FW**: We were chatting about school and getting ready for each day and we talked about a few ideas and how you'd like to help Ryan and Christie-Lee to improve their attendance. Can you remember some of the things we discussed?

**J**: Some of it. The bedtime thing and the star chart. We've not done that yet though.

**FW**: Ok, we can chat about that. Those were great ideas though. There were a few other things we discussed. Have you got the list we made? We could have a quick reminder if you like?

**J**: Yeah, it's on the fridge door.

**FW**: Shall we have a look?

**J**: I'll get it.

**FW**: Ok.

**J**: Here it is.

**FW**: Alright, so what have we got? What did we identify as good ideas?

**J**: Erm … we've got set bedtimes for the kids. And getting school clothes ready the night before. I've been doing that.

**FW**: Ok great. Let's go through the list we made first, then maybe we can identify what you've got going and a few things we might want to work on. Is that ok?

**J**: Ok.

**FW**: Alright, so what else did we include on the list.

**J**: Contacting school about the family learning thing. I'm a bit nervous about that though, I didn't get on with school. I know it's a good thing; just not sure. It might be good for me and Christie-Lee. I don't think Ryan likes the sound of that.

**FW**: That's ok Jenny, we can talk about that. I can help you find the right person to chat to you if you like. Let's see what else is on your list there …

**J**: Er … alarms set for 7 o'clock for Ryan and 7.15 for Christie-Lee.

**FW**: Ok, sounds good. You've got some other things there …

**J**: Breakfast stuff. Make sure there's bread for toast and some cereal. And milk. And make up their packed lunch the night before so I don't stress about it in the morning.

**FW**: Ok, great. And what's that about showers?

**J**: Make sure the kids have a shower every day. Morning best but the night before is more realistic cos they're hopeless in the morning.

**FW**: Well done, and …?

**J**: Having a treat for when they've been at school all week. But not money. Clean clothes for school. Clean shirts on Mondays, Wednesdays and Fridays. I've not done that cos I didn't have time this week. They had clean shirts on Monday though.

**FW**: Ok, I understand. What else did we list up as good ideas? No one is expecting you to do all these things straight away. It's good to have a list though isn't it?

**J**: Yeah, it's alright.

**FW**: What else did we chat about?

**J**: No TV in the mornings until they are dressed and having breakfast.

**FW**: Good idea.

**J**: And walk with Christie-Lee to the bus stop. Ryan wouldn't let me; he says he'd be too embarrassed. He's 11, you know.

**FW**: How old is Christie-Lee now?

**J**: She's 7; 8 in January.

**FW**: Ok. What were the other things you put on your list?

**J**: Oh, yeah, well, er … that I'd get up with the kids, at the same time, you know …

**FW**: I think that will make a huge difference. This is a really impressive list Jenny. They're sort of ambitions for you to work towards aren't they? So let's have a think about these things.

Jenny's planned strategies for achieving improved school attendance for her children (note the ambiguity of *improved*, by the way) will help, as she and her children will have a set of reference points to measure against. Jenny can review her own parental performance and identify what she is doing well, her *continue to*'s, and those things she has yet to make happen – her *begin to*'s. With these reference points in place we can now use Continue & Begin Fast Coaching.

**FW**: Which of them have you been able to start doing since the last time we chatted?

**J**: School clothes. I've been tidying them and making sure they're in the kids' bedroom before they go to sleep.

**FW**: That's great Jenny! They'll have them ready to put on the mornings – and no stress. What else have you been able to get going?

**J**: Showers. They both have a shower before bedtime. I thought about in the morning but I know it's not going to happen, so I thought at least they're having a wash each day.

**FW**: That's brill! Keep going – tell me some other things you've been doing. Think about the list we made together.

**J**: Breakfast. I've been going to the Co-op on Sunday nights. I've got enough Weetabix for the week and I bought a loaf, some milk and some crumpets. They last well. I got some honey too. Both the kids like honey on crumpets.

**FW**: Nice one Jenny! You've been planning the week. How much easier is that now? No need to stress about breakfast.

**J**: Yeah, I suppose so.

**FW**: This is a really good start. I'm so pleased for you. Ok, so tell me something else you're doing now that you weren't doing before.

**J**: I think that's about it, really. I've been getting on top of the washing but I haven't got the school shirts sorted yet, like we said – you know, clean ones on Mondays, Wednesdays and Fridays. I'm not that organised yet. Ryan's a nightmare for not putting his dirty shirts in the laundry basket.

**FW**: Have you got enough shirts?

**J**: At the moment we have. Ryan's growing though, we'll need new ones soon.

**FW**: Ok, we can have a word with school if you like; they can sometimes help with school uniform. I can ask, if you'd like me to?

**J**: That would be good … please.

**FW**: Ok. Tell me about morning alarms. Christie-Lee was just showing me hers.

**J**: Oh yeah. Well, I've got them both alarm clocks – I got them from the Pound shop. Ryan still didn't wake up on time yesterday so I had to call him. Christie-Lee did though. She has all week. We had breakfast together this morning.

**FW**: You woke him up? That's means …

**J**: Yeah, I've been getting up with them.

**FW**: Aww, that's lovely! It's great that you've been getting up with them too. It shows you care doesn't it? You've got some really impressive things up and running in your home now.

**J**: I got up every day except Wednesday. I was feeling a bit down, you know …

**FW**: Down in what way exactly?

**J**: I'm on medication for depression. Sometimes I find it difficult, you know … to cope, and I think I'm letting the kids down. They can be difficult though … you know?

**FW**: Does school know you've been feeling down? It might be worth letting someone know. If we need to we can talk to school about getting help to collect the kids, especially Christie-Lee. Sounds like you're doing well getting up with them though!

**J**: I'm doing ok. I got an alarm clock too. I went for pink, like Christie-Lee's!

**FW**: Ha ha! Ok, well, let's make the most of all these good things you're already doing to help your children. Let's celebrate what you've achieved. It really is impressive Jenny. Let's run through the things you've managed to get going in your family home. All of these things will help Ryan and Christie-Lee get to school on time and be ready for a full day of education. So, let's think … what did you say you are doing now? Let's list them quickly.

**J**: Er … making sure the school clothes are in their bedrooms, ready for school next morning.

**FW**: Yes, and …?

**J**: Both of them have been having a shower before bedtime. Christie-Lee goes first them Ryan. He's in there for ages.

**FW**: Ok.

**J**: I got breakfast stuff from the Co-op on Sunday evening so there's something every morning for them.

**FW**: Lovely.

**J**: Er …

**FW**: Alarms?

**J**: Oh yeah … we've been setting our alarms. I've been doing it too.

**FW**: Hooray! And that means …?

**J**: I've been getting up with the kids. Well, except Wednesday, like I said.

**FW**: Ok, yes I know. Hey, I'm so proud of you Jenny. You must be really pleased with what you've done in such a short period of time.

**J**: Yeah, I suppose so. I've got another idea though. I think we'll have a rule about no X Box after 9 p.m. Ryan's on it for hours. His bedroom light is off but I know he's playing on it.

**FW**: Ok, well we can have a think about that in a minute. It sounds like a good idea.

**J**: Yeah.

**FW**: Ok, shall we make a quick note of all these cool things you've been doing to help your children? Do you want to write them down or shall I?

**J**: Can you do it? My writing's not that good.

**FW**: No problem. Ok, you shout out and I'll make a note. What were they? Quickly … school clothes …

**J**: Yeah. Showers, breakfast, alarms …

**FW**: You got up …

**J**: Yeah.

**FW**: Amazing! There's five things you're already doing well to help your children get to school. So, would you like to continue to do those things with your children?

**J**: Yeah, of course.

**FW**: Ok, well, give yourself a pat on the back. This is really impressive Jenny, I think you can be super-proud of yourself. Super-mum skills!

**J**: Ha! Cheers.

**FW**: How does it feel?

**J**: Yeah, good.

**FW**: Quite right too. Ok, so you're going to carry one with these things, are you?

**J**: Yeah, I am.

**FW**: Cool. So, let's think about next steps then. What would you like to *begin to* do, that would support your children even more – things that would help them get back into school regularly? We had other things on your list.

**J**: Yeah, like I say, the X Box. I think we should have a rule about turning it off at 9 p.m.

**FW**: Ok, that makes sense. How will you make that happen?

**J**: Well, I need to talk to him.

**FW**: What will you say?

**J**: Don't know. Maybe something about wanting to help him and be a good parent, but I need him to help himself as well.

**FW**: Sounds good Jenny. What else have you got in mind for changing things? Remember the ideas we had earlier.

**J**: The star charts. I don't think it would work for Ryan you know; he might think it's a bit baby-ish. I think Christie-Lee would go for it though.

**FW**: Ok, that sounds good. What will you include in the star charts? What sort of things would you include?

**J**: I'm not sure yet. Maybe the obvious: getting to school on time – I suppose that would be getting to the bus stop on time, really. Maybe the shower each night – she's already doing it, it might just make her feel she's already doing well, you know …

**FW**: Good thinking. What else could you include?

**J**: Maybe that she's had some breakfast?

**FW**: That's a great idea. Star charts are great because you can give the kids a treat when they do well. It helps them feel a sense of achievement and that you have to work to get things. So, how will you make the star chart idea happen?

**J**: I'm going to ask Ryan to help me … you know, make one on the computer and print it off. He's good on the computer. He might want to help his little sister – something like that. Maybe I'll tease him about having his own star chart, or a more grown up one or something.

**FW**: Nice. How do you think you could introduce the idea to them?

**J**: I think that's the same kind of thing, you know … tell them both I want to be a good mum and do everything I can to get them to school and I need them to help me to help them. I'm trying to do my best as a single mum, you know. We can talk about it at teatime.

**FW**: You're doing really well here Jenny; that's two great things which will definitely help Christie-Lee and Ryan. You're doing great. What about the family learning idea?

**J**: I'd like to … not sure though. I think I'd be a bit … you know, embarrassed.

**FW**: Would it be helpful if you had a chat with school about how the family learning works? I know the team at St. Martin's really well. Their family learning programme is really successful. There are lots of parents getting involved now. Most mums and dads are a bit nervous when they start – that's normal, isn't it? It's so good for the kids though – it shows them how much you care about their education and what a good mum you are. Shall I get Dawn Bridger to give you call? She runs the scheme; she's lovely.

**J**: Ok, yeah.

**FW**: Alright, so, let's summarise: you identified three things you're going to *begin to* do differently from now on that will help Ryan and Christie-Lee improve their attendance at school and improve their education. What were they?

**J**: Er … Xbox. No Xbox after 9 p.m. A star chart for Christie-Lee and I'm going to ask Ryan to help make it.

**FW**: And a really cool thing you're going to find out about …?

**J**: The family learning thing. I'm still nervous though.

**FW**: That's ok. And I've promised to contact the lady at school – Dawn – and ask her to give you a call. Is that alright?

**J**: Yeah, ok, thanks.

**FW**: Alright. So, let's just fast-forward a bit – imagine you're continuing with all the good things you're already doing, you know, from the big list we made. What are the things you're already doing? Let's remind ourselves quickly …

**J**: Er …

**FW**: School clothes …

**J**: Yeah … er … showers. Getting the breakfast stuff on Sundays. Alarms …

**FW**: And you've been getting up.

**J**: Yeah.

**FW**: And you feel good about doing all those things, to help your children get to school, is that right?

**J**: Yeah, when you put it like that I suppose I do.

**FW**: Fantastic! You're already doing some great things! Super-mum skills! And you're going to continue to do those things?

**J**: Yeah, I am.

**FW**: Cool! And we've made a note of them so we can celebrate how brilliantly you're doing. And now you've decided on three new things you're going to start doing which will help your children even more, is that right?

**J**: Yeah.

**FW**: And what are they?

**J**: Er … no Xbox after 9. The star charts, and you're going to get Dawn What's-her-face to call me about the family learning thing.

**FW**: Hooray! What a plan! Ok, let's make a note of these as well. Still want me to do the writing?

**J**: Please.

**FW**: So, let's do the fast-forward thing. A few weeks' time, Ryan is turning his Xbox off at 9 o'clock each night, the star charts are in full swing, and you've been to the family learning sessions at St. Martin's with Christie-Lee; how will you be feeling?

**J**: Good. Yeah. I'll feel like we're making progress.

**FW**: You'd feel like you're making progress – that's cool. And what else would you feel?

J: Like I'm being a good mum for my children. And I'll feel proud too, I suppose. Like I'm doing the best for my kids and they are doing their bit for themselves. Yeah … yeah, it'd be good.

FW: Ok, so is this something you're going to do?

J: Yeah.

FW: Just checking, cos sometimes people talk about things but don't actually get on and do it.

J: No, I'll do it. I'll talk to the kids tonight.

FW: Excellent. Do you need any more help from me or anyone else?

J: Just the chatting to the lady from school, that's all. I can do the rest.

FW: Ok Jenny, this is really impressive. I'll leave you with the list we've just made – the *continue to*'s and the *begin to*'s. I've got my own notes here too. When would be a good time for us to catch up on this and see how you're getting on?

J: I dunno. When are you coming next?

FW: How about 2 weeks today?

J: Ok, I'll get some coffee in next time. That's not everything on the list though. We had other things to … you know … the clean shirts and that.

FW: That's ok Jenny. We can chat about that next time if you like.

## Example 2: Sport – teenage rugby player's skills development

Max is a talented 15-year-old rugby player. He plays for his school, his local club and represents his county, Hampshire, He plays full back, a key position within a rugby team.

A rugby full back positions himself/herself at the back of the field, playing as last line of defence against opposition runners and opponents' kicks. As a result, full backs are expected to have excellent defensive ball-catching, kicking and tackling skills. In attack, a good full back offers a threat as a strike runner, joining the line of players in unexpected and innovative positions, to surprise opponent defenders.

As a county player, Max has been introduced to specialist training to help him develop his full-back skills to even higher levels. In this fast coaching session he reflects on his most recent games and considers – and celebrates – those parts of his training he has been able to implement during the games. After celebration he considers change and how he could develop his game further by adopting more advanced skills and practices.

Terminology to be aware of:

- **Kicking out of hand**: when a player kicks the ball by dropping it from waist height, either to find the safety of the touchline for a restart, or as an attacking threat by kicking high into the opponents' half of the field, for fellow team members to chase and tackle the opponent gathering the ball.
- **Touch**: the touchline or 'touch' is the edge of the pitch on each side. When the ball crosses over the touchline the game is restarted by one team throwing the ball back onto the pitch. Players from both teams line up to jump and compete to catch the ball. This is known as a line-out.
- **Stinger**: a temporary and painful injury caused by over stretching a neck nerve, usually as a result of an awkward tackle. The stinger injury to the neck tends to occur when the head is pushed to one side and the shoulder is dropped down the other way. Players who have had stingers report pins and needles, or an electric shock, or sudden weakness in one arm. A stinger injury can be very short-lived thankfully, perhaps just a few minutes or in more serious instances, hours and days.
- **Fly half**: the controller of attacking moves, sometimes known as the '10' due to the shirt number worn. Max occasionally plays fly half and will be moving to that position more permanently next season.
- **Winger**: a fast runner, playing on the wide outside of the pitch. Wingers are usually fast runners who consequently score the majority of the tries in a game.
- **15**: Shirt number worn by the full back.

- **5-metre line, 22-metre line, halfway line, 10-metre line**: markings on the pitch 5 metres from defending try line, 22 metres from defending try line, half way, 10 metres from halfway line.
- **Gap**: a physical space between defending players that allows attacking runners to sprint forward with the ball, through a defensive line, without being tackled.
- **Kicking tee**: a plastic support for the ball, used to aid place kicking.

**Coach**: Alright Max, how's it going?

**Max**: Alright.

**Coach**: What did you think of the game?

**Max**: Not the best – it was ok. The weather didn't help.

**Coach**: That's true. Plenty of tries though, your Dad told me. 43–24 … a good win!

**Max**: Yeah, should have been more though. I got a stinger.

**Coach**: Yeah. How're you feeling now?

**Max**: It's ok, bit sore.

**Coach**: Any pins and needles? Weakness?

**Max**: Just a bit sore.

**Coach**: So, what did you think of your own game? In fact let's chat about recent games this season so far. What's been going well?

**Max**: Tackling has been good.

**Coach**: Oh ok, in what way?

**Max**: Good on my right shoulder. Side tackles, front-on tackles. I've been getting up on my feet again, back in the game.

**Coach**: Nice. How come you've been so good? What have you been doing differently?

**Max**: Just grown up I think, playing for Hampshire, the players are bigger. I've had to step up.

**Coach**: Sounds like some of that is in your mind? Deciding to step up ...

**Max**: Yeah ... had to think differently, faster.

**Coach**: Ok, cool. What else have you been doing well this season?

**Max**: Adapting positions, moving to fly half, and on the wing for Hampshire sometimes.

**Coach**: How've you gone about adapting?

**Max**: Just changing position. It's a bit different in each position, full back and winger are quite similar.

**Coach**: What do you do? Do you think about the new position before the game? Say anything to yourself?

**Max**: I think to myself I need to get the ball to the others, to help them to help me.

**Coach**: From 10?

**Max**: Yeah.

**Coach**: Ok, being adaptive like that is great. Tell me something else that's been going well for you.

**Max**: Kicking out of hand.

**Coach**: Oh, right? How've you been getting on with that then? In what way are you better?

**Max**: Yeah, good. I used to make touch from the 5-metre line to the 22. Now I can make halfway – even the 10-metre line in their half.

**Coach**: In their half?

**Max**: Yeah.

**Coach**: That's impressive!

**Max**: Yeah.

**Coach**: So how have you managed to do that? What's the structure you're using?

**Max**: Aiden's been helping me.

**Coach**: Your technical coach?

**Max**: Yeah.

**Coach**: What have you been working on with him?

**Max**: Where I place my feet; angle the ball, not my feet; kick through the ball; don't let the ball move through the air as you drop it onto your foot.

**Coach**: That's awesome Max!

**Max**: Yeah. I can kick off my right foot now too.

**Coach**: You a lefty?

**Max**. Yeah. My technique is better off my right. I learned the technique – not as much power though.

**Coach**: Alright. What else is going on for you so far this season?

**Max**: Footwork agility – I'm much better now.

**Coach**: In what way, specifically?

**Max**: Getting past people easier, in smaller gaps.

**Coach**: How come?

**Max**: I've been doing ladder work with Aiden. We've been using a grid system – the Illinois Agility Test.

**Coach**: Good?

**Max**: Yeah, really good.

**Coach**: Alright. More stuff you're pleased with?

**Max**: Er … communication is improving.

**Coach**: Communication … in what way?

**Max**: With teammates. I'm talking with them a lot more, calling them across to defend … at 15 … even more at 10.

**Coach**: Excellent. Sounds good. That's an impressive list of achievements so far this season Max. Let's just run through them, tackling …

**Max**: Yeah … adapting positions.

**Coach**: Yeah … kicking out of hand.

**Max**: Footwork agility.

**Coach**: Yeah … and …?

**Max**: Communication.

**Coach**: Nice. That's quite a list! Pleased with that? Feel good about yourself?

**Max**: Yeah … yeah.

**Coach**: Quite right too. Going to continue to do that stuff well?

**Max**: Yeah.

**Coach**: Superb. Let's make a note of them on the Continue & Begin action plan.

[**Max** notes down *continue to* behaviours]

**Coach**: Ok, so very impressive. Now, to get to the next level, to become even better, what do you want to start doing differently?

**Max**: Being quicker, to be there before the gap closes.

**Coach**: Alright, tell me about that, how are you going to do that?

**Max**: Sprint training – more of it – more agility work.

**Coach**: Anticipation work?

**Max**: Maybe. Just quicker off the mark – sprint training.

**Coach**: Ok, sprint training, that's cool. What else do you want to work on?

**Max**: Kicking off the tee – I'm a bit hit and miss.

**Coach**: Ok ... what's your plan?

**Max**: More practice. Loads and loads of practice.

**Coach**: Alright ... trial and error? Or guided practice? Or a bit of both?

**Max**: Bit of both I suppose. I need a set routine – Aiden can help. We start again after Christmas, once a week.

**Coach**: Good. So, there's a couple of things you're going to start doing differently Max, what are they?

**Max**: Being quicker, sprint training, more agility.

**Coach**: Yep, and ...?

**Max**: Kicking off the tee – guided practice with Aiden.

**Coach**: Alright. So tell me this Max, pretty soon you're going to be playing even better than you already are with these new skills in place. Being quicker to be there before the gap closes and improved kicking from the tee ... right?

**Max**: Yeah.

**Coach**: So ... what's that going to do for you? Being able to do those things really well? On top of the things you're already brilliant at?

**Max**: Make me better.

**Coach**: What's it going to make you feel?

**Max**: I'll enjoy it more. I'll feel confident.

**Coach**: Ok, well, would you like those feelings?

**Max**: Yeah!

**Coach**: Alright. So, let's get those *begin to*'s written down on the plan.

[**Max** adds the *begin to* ambitions to his action plan.]

**Coach**: Let's run through this from the start, really quick, the things you're already brilliant at.

**Max**: Tackling, adapting positions, kicking out of hand, footwork agility, communicating with the team.

**Coach**: Nice. Feel good about that?

**Max**: Yeah.

**Coach**: Quite right too. Impressive. And a couple of things you're going to start doing differently from now on that will make you even more impressive on a rugby field, and they are …?

**Max**: Quicker to the gap, kicking off the tee.

**Coach**: Excellent … and you have a plan to make both those things happen, right?

**Max**: Yeah.

**Coach**: Ok, and remind me, what will that do for you? How will you feel when you're doing those things really well? On top of the things you're already brilliant at?

**Max**: I'll feel better and I'll enjoy playing more. I'll be more confident.

**Coach**: Alright. And you'd like those feelings would you?

**Max**: Yeah.

**Coach**: Ok … so, I need to ask you this: is this something you're going to do? Or have we just been having a nice chat?

**Max**: I'm definitely doing it!

**Coach**: Ok. Well I'd better find out when your next game is so I can come and watch you in action!

**Max**: Yeah, alright. Cheers for that.

## Example 3: Call centre – inbound customer enquiries (telecoms industry)

In this scenario, Andy, a call centre agent, has just completed an inbound call from a customer. His coach (Bilan) listened in on the call. Bilan helps Andy celebrate his successes in relation to a set of explicit standards described in the call centre's operating procedures and which Andy learned during a recent training programme. It is his performance compared to these operating procedures that provide reference material for the fast coaching discussion.

**Bilan**: Hey Andy, I was listening to your call there, how do you think that went?

**Andy**: Really good, yes very good.

**Bilan**: Alright! Very good. In what way was it very good?

**Andy**: Well, I dealt with the reason for the customer's call, it was all dealt with and, yeah … I think he went off the call pretty happy.

**Bilan**: Yeah, he seemed to be didn't he? So let's go through it specifically – which elements of the call were you pleased with? And think about particular parts of the call.

**Andy**: I was very pleased I used the customer's name throughout the call.

**Bilan**: Yes, you used his name a lot didn't you?

**Andy**: Yeah, it makes a difference to the customer.

**Bilan**: Why is that do you think?

**Andy**: It's personal – it makes the customer feel like they are an individual, not just another caller.

**Bilan**: Very good, that was fabulous wasn't it? Ok, let's think about some other aspects. What else did you do there that was good?

**Andy**: I think overall the call was dealt with efficiently.

**Bilan**: Ok, efficient. What do you mean by efficient?

**Andy**: You know … I was as quick as I could be without rushing the customer or putting him under pressure.

**Bilan**: How specifically did you make it efficient?

**Andy**: I don't think they were on the call for any longer than they needed to be … you know … I spoke with the relevant departments for the issues that the customer had; they were all dealt with, so …

**Bilan**: All dealt with? Yeah, ok fabulous. So you had an efficient call, you used their name, what else went well? What else did you manage to do there?

**Andy**: I offered the package options to them.

**Bilan**: Yeah you did, and what were those package options?

**Andy**: Oh, mainly for this customer they were interested in the sports and movie channels. I think they were a couple of football and film fans.

**Bilan**: And you finished the call off. Can you remember how you finished the call off as well?

**Andy**: Enjoy the football.

**Bilan**: That was lovely wasn't it?

**Andy**: Yeah.

**Bilan**: Alright. Hey, what about rapport and that kind of stuff? How do you think you got on there?

**Andy**: Yeah, very good. Particularly when you just mentioned about the football, yeah … you know, as soon as they mentioned the sports and the movies I mentioned about are they sports fans, who they support and that kind of thing.

**Bilan**: You got into a great conversation with them about that didn't you?

**Andy**: Yeah.

**Bilan**: Alright. Fantastic, so we've got a big old list of things that went well as you identified, what are those? Run through again very quickly.

**Andy**: The use of the name.

**Bilan**: Name.

**Andy**: Yeah, the call was efficiently dealt with.

**Bilan**: Efficient, yes.

**Andy**: The package options.

**Bilan**: The package options, yep.

**Andy**: And I also offered help at the end the package options.

**Bilan**: Cool. And as well as that, throughout all the conversation there was plenty of …?

**Andy**: Plenty of rapport.

**Bilan**: And how did you do that, exactly?

**Andy**: We got chatting about the football.

**Bilan**: That's it, fantastic! You must be really pleased with that.

**Andy**: Yes, I'm very, very … it was a really good call.

**Bilan**: Ok. Well look, in the spirit of Continue & Begin let's make a note of those *continue to*'s. We'll put those on the action plan shall we?

**Andy**: Ok.

**Bilan**: Let's do that now.

[Andy writes his *continue to* successes on an action plan.]

**Bilan**: Ok, so we've got a fantastic set of *continue to*'s there Andy.

**Andy**: I think so, yeah.

**Bilan**: We can celebrate that and feel good. So let's just think, next time you're having a call like that, what do you think you might want to do, perhaps a little bit more differently, that would make that performance even better? Even more professional, what do you think?

**Andy**: Well, now that you've come to mention it, I think the one thing that I think would have been better and more efficient for the customer is for me to actually bring up the subject of the package options, instead of the customer asking for them first.

**Bilan**: Ask for them first, that's right … yeah.

**Andy**: I could maybe have proactively offered that first.

**Bilan**: Yeah, ok … yeah that's a smart idea, because they might not always question it, it's good to do that. Well, that makes a lot of sense. So that's something that you could *begin to* do from now on?

**Andy**: Definitely, yes.

**Bilan**: Oh, ok, let's think of something else. What else could you do that would make that performance even more professional?

**Andy**: Not sure …

**Bilan**: Ok, well, let's think about the training you had. Let's think about … [mimes keyboard typing]

**Andy**: Ah, of course, yeah. Online. Yes, that's something that I could have done – about the reason for this customer's call. I think a lot of it … they could have dealt with it online on the website.

**Bilan**: There we are.

**Andy**: And maybe it would have cut down on the call time too.

**Bilan**: Yeah, cut down on the call, which is good for you as well, I guess?

**Andy**: Absolutely, yes. I've got my metrics.

**Bilan**: Yeah, ok, is that something you could do from now on?

**Andy**: Promote online? Definitely, yes.

**Bilan**: How do you do that? What would have to happen? What would you say?

**Andy**: It's just making the customer aware that, while you're dealing with the issues of why they're calling, you could just bring that in: 'To save you waiting in the queue next time Mr Davis, are you aware that you can do this on our website?' That kind of thing.

**Bilan**: Yeah, that's nice isn't it? 'To save you waiting …' is really nice. Ok great, so we've got a couple of fabulous *begin to*'s. What are they again? First one was …?

**Andy**: The first one was proactively offer packages.

**Bilan**: That's right, yes, proactively offer packages. And the second one was?

**Andy**: Promote online service. I need to get to grips with that.

**Bilan**: Promote online service … you'll soon grasp that Andy, I'm sure. Alright, they're superb aren't they! Ok, so tell me Andy, when you're doing these things really well, how will you feel? What will it feel like doing these *begin to*'s?

**Andy**: Brilliant!

**Bilan**: In what way? How will it be brilliant? What will be going on for you?

**Andy**: Well, I'll feel like I'm doing my job really well, that I'm really helping the customer in the best way, that I'm being professional, you know …

**Bilan**: Nice! And you'd like to have those feelings would you? Feeling …?

**Andy**: Professional.

**Bilan**: Yes, professional. You'd like that feeling?

**Andy**: Yes, I would.

**Bilan**: Ok, cool. Shall we make a note of those *begin to*'s on the action plan? In the *begin to* section?

**Andy**: Yeah!

**Bilan**: Ha ha! Ok, let's do that.

[Andy writes his *begin to* ambitions on his action plan.]

**Bilan**: Ok, Andy, so we've got a great action plan there; we've got a big old list of *continue to*'s and a couple of *begin to*'s. Let's run through them again very, very quickly. What are the things you're going to *continue to* do well?

**Andy**: The use of the customer's name, to deal with the calls efficiently as I can, to offer package help, ask if they need any more help at the end of the call.

**Bilan**: Offering more help at the end of the call is nice isn't it?

**Andy**: Yes.

**Bilan**: Yes. And woven all the way through it was …?

**Andy**: Was the rapport.

**Bilan**: The rapport was super wasn't it? Right, so you're really pleased with that?

**Andy**: Very, yes.

**Bilan**: Feeling good about being professional with those things?

**Andy**: Yes, I do.

**Bilan**: Ok. And we've identified two things that you're going to start doing a little bit differently from now on to make your performance even better, even more professional. And what are those two things?

**Andy**: The first one was to proactively offer the package help, rather than to wait for the customer to raise it.

**Bilan**: Right yeah, and the second one was?

**Andy**: Promoting online.

**Bilan**: Promoting online, and what will that do for you? Making those two *begin to*'s happen? Proactively offering the package and promoting online help.

**Andy**: I'll feel I'm being really professional.

**Bilan**: Nice feeling?

**Andy**: Yeah, definitely.

**Bilan**: You'd like that?

**Andy**: Of course!

**Bilan**: Well, alright then! Ok, well they're fabulous *begin to*'s and you've got a great plan. Now I need to check the *begin to*'s … are you going to be able to implement those things?

**Andy**: I think so. Yes I think so.

**Bilan**: Think so? Do you need any help? Or is it something you can do yourself?

**Andy**: It's something I can do myself, yeah.

**Bilan**: Alright, I just need to check you are going to do these things.

**Andy**: Most definitely, yes.

**Bilan**: Ok. Alright, it's a wonderful plan, now I'm going to be back here this time next week I guess.

**Andy**: Ok.

**Bilan**: Would it be useful for us to get together and see how you're getting on with the *continue to*'s, and of course the *begin to*'s?

**Andy**: Most definitely, yeah. That would be fantastic, yes.

**Bilan**: Yeah, I would like to see you again.

**Andy**: Yeah, good … thanks.

**Bilan**: Alright, we'll see each other next week and we'll go through this, shall we?

**Andy**: Brilliant … thank you, yeah.

**Bilan**: Congratulations Andy.

**Andy**: Thank you very much!

**Bilan**: Great to see you, take care of yourself.

**Andy**: Thanks Bilan, you too.

## Example 4: Big ticket retail – understanding the customer

In this scenario Jamie, a kitchen, bedroom and bathroom (KBB) sales consultant is being coached to celebrate a series of *continue to* behaviours in the kitchen showroom, followed by a commitment to implement two key *begin to* ambitions. His coach has watched and listened to his performance – observed behaviour – with a prospective customer. In the KBB sector a 'close' is either a sale or, as a stepping stone to the close, an agreement from the customer to continue the buying conversation in her home, at a time and date to be agreed. Jamie secures an appointment at the customer's home as the close in this example.

The illustration includes a number of technical sales words and phrases. These are described in brief, to aid understanding of how *New Code* Continue & Begin Fast Coaching was used in this instance:

- **Truism**: a statement of obvious truth that cannot be denied; used by sales professionals to begin conversations.
- **Price acceptance map**: an idea of likely customer spend.
- **Qualification**: asking questions to understand the customer's requirements.
- **Up-to**: a question asked to understand potential movement on likely spend.

**Coach**: Alright Jamie, so I was just watching you and listening to you with that customer there. How do you think that went?

**Jamie**: Yeah, I think it went really well.

**Coach**: Ok, in what way? What specifically was good do you think?

**Jamie**: Well, I think the approach – how I approached the customer – went really well.

**Coach**: Ok cool. What was it that you did, specifically?

**Jamie**: Traditional big smile.

Coach: Ok, yeah …

Jamie: Big warm welcome, sort of showed her the showroom, so yeah …

Coach: Big warm welcome – how, specifically …?

Jamie: I thanked her for coming in, open gestures, mentioned the sunny weather – a truism I suppose.

Coach: Lovely, It was a nice warm welcome, wasn't it? Ok, alright, so let's celebrate that. I was thinking about some other things that went well. Think back to the training programme 'Helping Customers Buy' – those five steps. Which elements of those five steps do you think you illustrated well there?

Jamie: I would say qualification … questions … trying to identify her needs.

Coach: Ok and how did you do that? How did you go about doing that?

Jamie: Trying to find out her usage.

Coach: Alright.

Jamie: The sort of style she's after, what sort of things she might be using the kitchen for.

Coach: What she's going to use it for, who's going to use it, yeah ok.

Jamie: Yeah I did that quite well.

Coach: And why. You asked her why she was thinking of changing her kitchen. Can you remember what she said?

Jamie: Yeah, It was to do with her children. They've moved away now to uni; she's got her house back so she wants a fresh start.

Coach: A fresh start, ok lovely … ok great. So what else went well do you think?

**Jamie:** The price acceptance map. That felt good.

**Coach:** Felt good, yeah that worked smoothly. What happened there?

**Jamie:** So, just trying to identify her investment in the project … so one of the questions I asked was, 'How much are you considering investing in your new kitchen?' which I think is a great question and she gave me an amount.

**Coach:** Yeah ok, and what was the number?

**Jamie:** £12,000.

**Coach:** Alright and then you asked something amazing. Do you remember what it was?

**Jamie:** Oh yeah, the up-to question.

**Coach:** Yeah, how did it go?

**Jamie:** I managed to stretch her investment to £15,000.

**Coach:** Ah wow! How about that?

**Jamie:** Yeah, it was brilliant.

**Coach:** Very cool indeed. Alright, let's think about some other things, what else went well?

**Jamie:** Um … I don't think I can …

**Coach:** Alright let's think about the five steps – the final step.

**Jamie:** Yeah … closing.

**Coach:** Yes, and what was the close for you here? What was it, specifically?

**Jamie:** What I tried to do is obviously get a site visit booked in, so we can go out and see the sort of things she like – obviously map out the kitchen. So yeah, I just asked her for a site visit and try and find a convenient day for her.

**Coach**: Ok and you managed to get one, fantastic. When was it?

**Jamie**: Thursday.

**Coach**: How about that! Ok so we've got some fabulous *continue to*'s. Lets run through again very quickly, things that you were pleased with.

**Jamie**: The approach – so, meet and greet.

**Coach**: Yeah that was cool wasn't it?

**Jamie**: Yeah, the qualification questions, the price acceptance.

**Coach**: The price acceptance map.

**Jamie**: … and then the up-to.

**Coach**: The up-to! How cool was that?

**Jamie**: Yeah that was great – and the close.

**Coach**: Yes, you closed to get the site visit. How about that? That's fabulous. So we can celebrate that and feel good about it. In the spirit of Continue & Begin, let's get those written down in the action plan. Let's do it.

**Jamie**: Yeah, ok.

[Jamie enters his *continue to* behaviours onto the action plan document.]

**Coach**: Right Jamie, so we've got some great *continue to*'s down on your action plan there. Let's think now about if you were in that situation again, next time round, what do you think you would do a little bit differently? That would make that performance with the customer even better?

**Jamie**: I think one of the things would probably have been the essentials, the desirable questions. Try to identify the essential things she needs. Yeah, that would have been good.

**Coach**: Oh ok, that's a smart move, isn't it. So you can get those things – the needs, the essentials – and differentiate those with the things that are aspirational – the things that she'd really like to have if she could.

**Jamie**: Yeah.

**Coach**: Smart move. That's something that you can do next time around is it?

**Jamie**: Definitely, yeah.

**Coach**: It fits in with those five steps doesn't it, part of that training programme. Alright, tell me something else you would like to do differently next time?

**Jamie**: Um …

**Coach**: Think about 'demonstration', 'features', 'benefits', 'feelings' and …?

**Jamie**: Yeah, so one of the things I probably could have done is sort of related back to what she said earlier, which was that she wants the space for entertainment again, and I think I could have probably shown some of the things that would work in a social, entertainment-type kitchen. I definitely could have linked that back to that qualification.

**Coach**: Oh, ok. That would be a great thing to do in the future, it's a really elegant skill to use – that would be fantastic. Ok … hey Jamie we've got a great couple of *begin to*'s, so let's just remind ourselves … the first one was?

**Jamie**: The first one was going through the essentials and the desirables, and then the second one was relating the features, benefits and feelings back to the qualification questions and what she wants to use the kitchen for.

**Coach**: Yeah fantastic … and these are things that you can do?

**Jamie**: Definitely.

**Coach**: Cool. So tell me, so, just imagine, in the near future, how will you feel when you're doing these two *begin to*'s really elegantly with customers, really professionally – how's that going to feel for you?

**Jamie**: That would be great. I'd feel good definitely.

**Coach**: Feel good … in what way?

**Jamie**: Like you said, professional. I'd feel I was really doing my job well. I'd feel confident and in control … good feelings.

**Coach**: Yes, they are good feelings. And would you like that – those feelings?

**Jamie**: Yes, I would.

**Coach**: Ok, so do you need any help with these *begin to*'s? Or is this something you can sort out on your own?

**Jamie**: I can definitely do it on my own.

**Coach**: Alright cool. Hey, well look … make sure that we get that stuff down on your action plan as well; it's really important. So, if you want to make a note of those on the Continue & Begin action plan.

**Jamie**: Yep.

[Jamie completes the *begin to* section of his action plan.]

**Coach**: Alright Jamie, so we've got a great action plan here. Let's just run through it again quickly. What have you got here?

**Jamie**: So, things that went well was the approach, the qualification, the price map … price acceptance map, the up-to.

**Coach**: The up-to was great wasn't it?

**Jamie**: It was great, and then the close.

**Coach**: And then the close. Alright fantastic ... and these are things that you're pleased with and that you're going to continue to do in the future?

**Jamie**: Definitely.

**Coach**: Let's celebrate that Jamie – congratulations. And as well as that we've got a couple of things that we are going to *begin to* do a little bit differently – and what are they?

**Jamie**: They are the essentials and desirables, so trying to identify those in the questioning.

**Coach**: Trying?

**Jamie**: Sorry, yes, I will be identifying the essentials and desirables, and the features and benefits and feelings, and linking those back to the qualification.

**Coach**: Linking it back to the qualification. You've done all of that good work with the qualification process it would be a shame not to make use of that wouldn't it? And it's good for the customer. Alright so we've got a fabulous plan, now I've got to ask you this: is this something you're going to do or has this just been an interesting conversation?

**Jamie**: Definitely, very serious about it.

**Coach**: Alright, nice. And do you need help to do that or can you do this stuff on your own?

**Jamie**: Definitely do it on my own.

**Coach**: Yeah? What has to happen to make these things happen?

**Jamie**: I just have to think it through carefully. I've got most of the sales process boxed off, I'll remember these two things after today.

**Coach**: You're right; you have got most of the sales process boxed off.

**Jamie**: Yeah, definitely.

**Coach**: Ok, and just remind me, what will you be feeling when you've got these two *begin to*'s boxed off as well, when you're doing these two things really elegantly – what did you say?

**Jamie**: I'll feel good, professional, doing my job well, confident.

**Coach**: You said 'control'.

**Jamie**: Yes, feeling like I'm in control of the sales process.

**Coach**: Alright then. So now I'm going to be back round here next week. How about we get together and find out – celebrate the fact I hope – you're *continuing to* do those things well and to see how you're getting on with those couple of *begin to*'s with customers? Would that be ok?

**Jamie**: Yeah, brilliant, that would be great.

**Coach**: Well, I will see you same time next week.

**Jamie**: Thank you very much.

**Coach**: Yeah, good on you Jamie!

## Example 4: Family coaching – helping Mum and going to school

Continue & Begin Fast Coaching is content-free, that is, the model is a framework through which we can address a diverse range of people development issues.

Here is an example of Continue & Begin Fast Coaching in use in the context of a 'troubled family', a focus for local authorities in the UK. This Continue & Begin Fast Coaching illustration involves a parent (Mum), an adolescent child (Jade) and their key worker from the multi-agency team supporting the family.

Jade is 12. She has been absent from school on numerous occasions, with her whereabouts unknown. When she is at school she has been disruptive. At home, where she lives with just her mum, she has previously been remote and disengaged, not communicating with her mother. Mum has some difficulty with mobility, although not registered disabled.

Because of historic issues in the family, support has been made available to Jade and her mum in the form of a key worker. A goal is to build cohesion in the family unit and a framework of behaviours for Jade and her mum to live by. So far, little has been agreed in the form of family rules or ambitions.

The key worker conducts this Continue & Begin coaching session with the principles of the UK Government's *Every Child Matters* policy in mind. *Every Child Matters* applies to the well-being of children and young people from when they're born until they reach the age of 19 and is based on the idea that every child, regardless of their individual circumstances or background, should have plenty of support throughout their life.

There are five key principles to the policy, which the UK Government believes children should have support with. These are:

1. to be healthy;
2. to stay safe;
3. to enjoy and achieve;
4. to make a positive contribution;
5. to achieve economic well-being.

A child should be healthy and stay safe. They should enjoy their childhood and achieve personal goals. Attainment in school is a stepping stone towards achieving these ambitions. For some children, gaining qualifications and employment is a route out of poverty.

This is a tricky Continue & Begin coaching session to manage as the coach has the above broad principles in mind, while no pre-agreed, explicitly described ambitions for the family to refer to are in place. Family rules evolve as the coaching conversation develops. This is Continue & Begin on the hoof and is inevitably restrictive in terms of outputs. Developing a set of family reference points is the pre-work to conducting subsequent high-performing Continue & Begin Fast Coaching sessions.

In some family coaching cases this is an inescapable starting point.

**Key Worker**: Good to see you both. So, how've you been getting on?

**Mum**: Still can't get her up for school in the morning – she's a nightmare!

**KW**: Oh, ok. What's been happening?

**Mum**: She spends all night on Facebook or watching TV and then she's too tired to get up for school.

**KW**: Mmm … ok. Well let's park that for a minute. What's been going on in a good way?

**Mum**: What do you mean?

**KW**: What's happened that's been positive – that you've both been pleased with – over the last week or so?

**Mum**: I dunno.

**KW**: What about you, Jade?

**Jade**: Dunno.

**KW**: Well, let's have a think. What has Jade done this week that's been a step in the right direction for you both?

**Mum**: Well, I suppose she's come in on time and she sat down to tea with me on Friday, which was nice.

**KW**: What time is 'on time'?

**Mum**: 6 o'clock, that's when I get tea ready.

**KW**: That's great. And what other positive things have been going on?

**Mum**: We've got on a bit better, haven't we? I mean we actually had a proper chat on Friday. We had a family dinner – with no arguments!

**KW**: Yeah? That's great! Family dinners are important. Tell me some more about your week.

**Mum**: She helped around the house a bit, didn't you Jade, and I can see the floor of her bedroom now – the first time ever!

**Jade**: It's not that bad!

**KW**: How did you help around the house Jade? What have you been doing?

**Jade**: Umm … I changed my bed and helped Mum with the washing on Sunday.

**KW**: I bet that was helpful for your mum. So things are progressing. Let's just remind ourselves, what's gone well this week? Remind me.

**Mum**: She's been coming in on time. At 6 o'clock.

**KW**: That's right, and …?

**Mum**: Sat down to tea as a family on Friday.

**Jade**: … and we had a chat.

**KW**: You had a chat.

**Mum**: … and you helped when you made your own bed and helped me with the washing on Sunday.

**KW**: Wow! That's four pieces of good news!

**Mum**: Four, yes.

**KW**: How do you feel about that Jade?

**Jade**: Good I suppose.

**KW**: Very good! Can you keep that up this week? Make it the norm?

**Jade**: What?

**KW**: Coming in by 6 o'clock, eating dinner together on Friday – which Mum makes – and you have a good chat, catch up on all the gossip, and you help around the house a little bit with changing your own bed, and helping Mum with the washing on Sunday?

**Jade**: S'pose so.

**KW**: That would be a real help for your mum. You could make it like these are things you and Mum agree to do. What do you think?

**Jade**: Yeah.

**KW**: How do think things at home might improve for you even more Jade? Things you'd like to be different? To change, maybe?

**Jade**: Dunno.

**KW**: Mum and you are a family; it's a small family, but you're still a family, and in families it helps if everyone gets a say in how things are managed. Would you like something to be different for you Jade? Or something for Mum to do differently?

**Jade**: [No response.]

**KW**: What about you Mum? What could you do to help you and Jade get along better as a family?

**Mum**: Not sure what you mean.

**KW**: How about the way you show interest in Jade, especially what's happening at school and with her friends?

**Mum**: I *am* interested.

**KW**: I'm sure you are. How could you show that, so Jade feels ok to chat with you about what's happening in her life?

**Mum**: We can talk about things at tea time every day. There's always people hanging around in the flat though.

**KW**: Ok, what can you do about that? About the people hanging around in the flat?

**Mum**: I suppose we could say: 'No one here while we have tea.'

**KW**: Well, that's an idea isn't it? Family time, eh?

**Mum**: Yeah, ok.

**KW**: What else could you do to help you and Jade get along well as mother and daughter, do you think?

**Mum**: We talked about doing some crafting together, cards – I've got loads of materials we could use. We thought about making birthday cards and Christmas cards, get well cards, that sort of thing, didn't we Jade?

**Jade**: Yeah, my friend Natalie does them. She sells them at craft fairs.

**KW**: That sounds a great idea! What has to happen to make that happen? To get it going?

**Mum**: We were going to chat about it on Friday, get the stuff out of the cupboard, see what we've got.

**KW**: Wow! That's exciting! Let me know how you get on.

**Mum**: Ok, we will.

**KW**: Ok, let's chat about school for a moment.

**Mum**: Getting her to actually go to school – and to stay there – that's the main problem.

**KW**: Ok, well ... yes, of course, school attendance is important. Going to school more regularly would be a good start, wouldn't it? How could that happen do you think? Jade?

**Jade**: I don't like it.

**KW**: Ok, what is it you don't like? Is there something specific you don't like?

**Jade**: [No response.]

**KW**: Well, what could we do to help you feel better about going?

**Jade**: I don't know. I don't like my form tutor. I want to move classes.

**KW**: What is it about him you don't like? Something specific?

**Jade**: He's a dick, just criticises all the time, like you're a 5-year-old. I can't stand him, he's such an idiot. I want to change classes or I'm not going, I hate him, Mr. Dickinson – we just call him Mr. Dick.

**KW**: Well, we can ask about changing forms, can't we?

**Jade**: I know a boy that moved classes when he asked.

**KW**: Ok, well, if Mum was to go into school and chat this through with the teachers, would you like that? See what school can do to help? I can come with you as support if you like Mum?

**Mum**: That would be good.

**KW**: Jade? What do you think?

**Jade**: Ok, yeah.

**KW**: Ok, so if we do this together, all three of us, and we managed to change classes, or maybe we find another way of making school better for you, would you promise to go to school?

**Jade**: Yeah.

**KW**: It sometimes helps if students have an identified member of staff to talk to. Who is someone you'd feel comfortable talking to at school, Jade?

**Jade**: Mrs Griffin … she's nice.

**KW**: Well then, let me give school a call when I get back to the office and see if we can get things moving. Mum, it would help if you took ownership of this now. If I give you a call and let you know who to speak to, will you arrange to go in to school? A bit of notice and I'll be able to come with you. Ok?

**Mum**: Yes, ok. I do want Jade to do well at school. I know it's important for the future, you know. We just got into this … you know, we've got sort of stuck.

**KW**: Well this can be a fresh start, can't it? I'll help with this Jade, if you promise to go to school on Monday and stay all day, even though you don't like your form tutor. Will you do that?

**Jade**: Dunno.

**KW**: That's the deal Jade.

**Jade**: Ok then.

**KW**: Is that a promise?

**Jade**: Yeah.

**KW**: It means staying all day and not being disruptive. Can you do that?

**Jade**: Yeah.

**KW**: If you were going to school regularly and you were enjoying school, how would that help do you think?

**Jade**: Dunno.

**KW**: How do you think you'd feel if you were getting on in school and attending regularly?

**Jade**: Good I suppose. I like being with my friends.

**KW**: Ok, well let's work towards that shall we? What do you think you'd like to do when you leave school?

**Jade**: I want to be a designer.

**KW**: Oh wow! What sort of design work?

**Jade**: Dunno; I like all sorts of designs.

**KW**: Well there's plenty of choice there. Design work is so interesting; there are so many paths you could take with that one.

**Jade**: Yeah.

**KW**: Ok, let's just remind ourselves of the progress we've made. What are the good things you and Mum have done in the last week Jade?

**Jade**: Er …

**KW**: Come in on time.

**Jade**: Oh yeah.

**KW**: And …?

**Jade**: Oh yeah, and sat down for tea and me and Mum had a chat about stuff.

**Mum**: And you helped me so much on Sunday with the bedding and the washing – I really appreciated your help.

**KW**: And are these things you think you'll continue to do?

**Jade**: Yeah.

**KW**: And Mum, what's happening on Friday evening?

**Mum**: Er …

**KW**: Crafting?

**Mum**: Oh yeah, we're going to get the craft materials out and start doing some making together.

**KW**: That's great! Ok, well I'll get on and contact the school, and Mum you'll make a call into school once I let you know who to speak to, when to call and all that, ok?

**Mum**: Ok, thanks.

**KW**: And Jade, me and Mum will do this stuff if you promise you'll go to school on Monday, and stay there all day.

**Jade**: Ok then.

**KW**: Promise?

**Jade**. Yeah.

**KW**: By the way, what will have to happen for you to go to school? To get up on time and be ready on Monday?

**Jade**: Got to get up.

**KW**: How can you make sure you will?

**Jade**: Alarm on my phone.

**KW**: Ok, what about uniform?

**Jade**: I'll get it ready Sunday. It's ok, I can get up if I have to – I'm not a baby.

**KW**: And Mum, will you promise to make sure Jade has clean uniform ready for her on Sunday evening?

**Mum**: I will – clean and crisp on the kitchen table for you Jade.

**KW**: Alright, well that sounds good doesn't it! And remind me, what will it feel like when you're back in school with your friends and you're attending regularly?

**Jade**: It'd be good. I like being with my friends, we have a laugh. I want to go, it's just the form tutor.

**KW**: Ok, well I've made a promise to you that I'll contact the school about that. Your promise is important though.

**Jade**: What?

**KW**: To go to school until we can sort that out for you.

**Jade**: Ok.

**KW**: Alright Mum, I've made a note of all those good things you and Jade are sharing together now. Here it is … keep it safe – fridge magnets are good for this. Jade coming in by 6 o'clock for tea, eating dinner together on Friday – which you make Mum – and you have a good chat, catch up on all the gossip about school and friends, and Jade … you'll continue to help around the house a little bit with changing your own bed and helping your mum with the washing on Sunday – these are things you're already doing! Hooray! And you're going to continue to do them together. Mum?

**Mum**: Yes.

**KW**: Jade?

**Jade**: Yeah.

**KW**: Alright! That's lovely to be doing those things already, and a few things we agreed you'll both do from now on – Mum?

**Mum**: Contact the school when you tell me who to speak to.

**KW**: Good. And something you're going to do together?

**Mum**: Crafting!

**KW**: Yep. And the one thing you're going to do with uniform?

**Mum**: I'll make sure it's all clean and crisp on Sunday evening. I'll leave it on the kitchen table.

**KW**: And you'll be at school on Monday morning Jade? On time, best behaviour, a full day at school, and I'll get on this afternoon and find out who the best person is for Mum to call. It might be Mrs Griffin or it might be someone else. Is that ok?

**Jade**: Yeah, thanks.

**KW**: Deffo?

**Jade**: Deffo.

**KW**: Alright. Hey, so let's think about the future. You're attending school, studying hard, doing well, enjoying yourself, having a good time with your friends, and you've just done well in an exam – how will you be feeling do you think?

**Jade**: Yeah, good.

**KW**: You'll be an awesome designer Jade! Get those exams sorted and – watch out design world, here comes Jade!

**Jade**: Ha! Right!

**KW**: Ok, I'll pop round on Monday evening and we can catch up on how we've all got on.

**Jade**: Ok, yeah. Cool.

**KW**: I've got to go! Thanks for the cuppa!

# *New Code* Can't to Can Belief Busting

### Example 1: Healthcare – time and personal management

Sam is a busy and stressed middle manager in a major hospital. He is responsible for the management of a range of projects and organisational deliverables, all of which have key performance indicators designed to measure and encourage successful implementation. Each project has regular review meetings, which are required to provide detailed reports and have a deep understanding of detail. He is regularly asked detailed questions for which he is expected to provide full answers. Sam is finding it difficult to allocate sufficient time to preparation for the project meetings. He also has administrative responsibilities for helping out-patients with financial queries. As a consequence he is feeling stressed and frustrated.

**Sam**: This is ridiculous; I don't have time for this.

**Nick**: For what mate?

**Sam**: These project meetings. I've got a project meeting at 11.30 and I've done absolutely zero reading prep for it and I don't know how I'm going to get this done. I've got patients waiting for me. I'm stacked out.

**Nick**: Ok … hey, what if you did have time?

**Sam**: Well that's a nice idea, but I don't have time so …

**Nick**: Ok, ok. Now just bear with me for a minute, let's just think this through, if you did have time to do the prep and go to these project meetings, right?

**Sam**: Yeah.

**Nick**: If you did have time to do the prep and the project meetings, what would that do for you? How would that help?

**Sam**: I don't have time though Nick.

**Nick**: Just pretend – go with me on this – some future time and place when you do have plenty of time to prep, how what that be for you?

**Sam**: Well it would be great. I mean, yeah, I wouldn't feel like I do now. I feel completely stressed out.

**Nick**: What's the opposite feeling, opposite of being completely stressed out?

**Sam**: I'd feel relaxed.

**Nick**: Ok, alright, and what other things would you feel? Good things?

**Sam**: Yeah, confident and not like … yeah …

**Nick**: Not like you are now! Ok, alright … you would like those feelings of, what did you say? What were the things that it would do for you?

**Sam**: Free up my time so I didn't feel stressed out – and confident and relaxed.

**Nick**: And you'd like that, yeah?

**Sam**: Of course.

**Nick**: Alright hey, well look, let's just think about it, what would have to happen for you to find time to be able to do the prep and the project meetings? What would have to happen?

**Sam**: I'd have to work faster, but I can't. I'm already absolutely stacked out, working flat out as I possibly can.

**Nick**: Alright, what other options have you got?

**Sam**: What do you mean?

**Nick**: What are the possible choices for you to have more time?

**Sam**: Well, I've got to stop doing one of these things basically.

**Nick**: Ok, alright. Well let's think about that. So what would have to happen for you to be able to stop doing one of these things? What could you do? What's involved?

**Sam**: I've got to drop something.

**Nick**: Well, what would have to happen for you to be able to drop something?

**Sam**: Well, I need to identify what I can drop – you know – but everything is urgent, everything needs to be done yesterday, so …

**Nick**: Ok I understand that, and how are you going to do that?

**Sam**: What?

**Nick**: Identify what to drop.

**Sam**: Well, I mean, a lot of the admin stuff that I do is completely unnecessary, and no one reads my reports anyway, but I suppose I'll have to write a list.

**Nick**: And what are you going to do with the list?

**Sam**: I suppose I have to take it to my manager.

**Nick**: Alright, and what's she going to say?

**Sam**: She'll ask for a proposal, she always does.

**Nick**: Ok … well that's understandable isn't it? So what I think you're saying is that in order for you to be able to drop something you've got to see your manager and put forward some proposal to her, is that right?

**Sam**: Yeah.

**Nick**: Ok, and you were thinking about putting a list together?

**Sam**: Yeah, I need to make a list.

**Nick**: Ok cool, so let's just think it through. In order for you to get the list, and the proposals that your manager's going to want, what have you got to do?

[Pause.]

**Sam**: Sit down and write a list.

**Nick**: Alright, well that's cool isn't it? It seems like the sensible thing to do. So when do you think you'll be able to do that?

**Sam**: Well, you know, I can do it soon.

**Nick**: Soon? Ok, so when specifically do you think you'll do that?

**Sam**: This week, definitely this week.

**Nick**: Ok, come on Sam, let's get specific. When are you going to do this? This week is a big old week. Because if you don't make a time and a date, it isn't going to happen is it? When are you going to do it?

**Sam**: Ok, fair enough, I can do it this afternoon.

**Nick**: What time?

**Sam**: Eh? Er … just before I … er … finish.

**Nick**: Give me a time, Sam!

**Sam**: Quarter to 5.

**Nick**: Ok fantastic, alright. So let's just see if I got this right: at quarter to 5 you're going to sit down, you're going to make a list of all of those admin tasks that you do and some proposals about which ones, specifically, you think you could drop so that you can take that to your line manager and you can chat through with her about your ideas, about what has to happen for you to drop them, and that will give you time – see if I've got this right – so it gives you time to do your prep, to go fully prepared to those project meetings. Is that right?

**Sam**: Yeah.

**Nick**: Yeah, ok, and what's that going to do for you?

**Sam**: You know, relieve some of this pressure so I don't feel so much stress.

**Nick**: And the flip side of not feeling stressed?

**Sam**: Relaxed, confident.

**Nick**: And you would like those feelings, is that right?

**Sam**: Yeah.

**Nick**: Ok, have we got a plan?

**Sam**: Sounds like a plan.

**Nick**: Alright, are you serious about it?

**Sam**: Yeah.

**Nick**: Need any help? Or can you do it on your own?

**Sam**: I can do it.

**Nick**: Alright, ok. Well, how about I meet up with you tomorrow to find out how you got on with preparing your list?

**Sam**: Alright yeah.

**Nick**: See you in a bit.

**Sam**: See you in a bit; I've got to go to this meeting!

## Example 2: Supported housing – breaking through beliefs about work

Matthew is a personal budgets officer for a housing provider, working directly with individual residents and tenants. Part of his role is to support residents in their management of personal finances, including debt management and rent payments. He has a wider remit to encourage self-determination and personal responsibility; to encourage personal growth and independence. In this Can't to Can conversation, Matthew is helping Elaine break through her limiting beliefs about gaining some form of employment.

**Matthew**: Hi Elaine, so what's on your mind?

**Elaine**: Just really fed up. I've got no money, can't get any work at all.

**Matthew**: Oh ok, feeling fed up is rubbish. What would happen if you could get work?

**Elaine**: What do you mean?

**Matthew**: What would it do for you if you actually could get work?

**Elaine**: Yeah, but I can't though, I just said.

**Matthew**: I know you say you can't, but just bear with me. What would you do if you actually were working?

**Elaine**: I don't know.

**Matthew**: I know you don't know, but if you did know, how do you think you would feel if you were in a job? If you were employed?

**Elaine**: Well I'd have some money.

**Matthew**: Right, what else would it do for you?

**Elaine**: Like what?

**Matthew**: How you'd feel being in work.

**Elaine**: Well … suppose I would feel a bit better about myself, and I'd be able to support my family a bit better.

**Matthew**: Would you like that?

**Elaine**: Well of course I would, but companies don't want people like me do they?

**Matthew**: Hang on a minute, let's just think this through for a while. Just imagine if you had a job that you got up to everyday, you left work at the end of the day – how would that make you feel?

**Elaine**: Well, yeah, I suppose it'd give me some more confidence, which I … I really need. It would take the pressure of my partner and I could take the kids out a bit more.

**Matthew**: Cool. Would you like that?

**Elaine**: Obviously.

**Matthew**: Ok, so to get some work, what would have to happen?

**Elaine**: Yeah but I can't.

**Matthew**: Hey, come on, we're exploring ideas, that's all. What's got to happen for you to get work, right now? What will you have to do?

**Elaine**: I suppose I'm going to have to start applying for jobs.

**Matthew**: Ok, and what would have to happen for that to take place?

**Elaine**: What do you mean?

**Matthew**: You know, start applying for jobs.

**Elaine**: Well … but no one's going to employ me.

**Matthew**: Let's just play it through, what has to happen for you to apply for a job?

**Elaine**: Well, I don't really know where to start, but I suppose a CV.

**Matthew**: Right, and how can you go about writing a CV?

**Elaine**: I don't know. Do the Jobcentre help with CV writing and interview skills? I could try there.

**Matthew**: Oh, ok … excellent. How could we make that happen?

**Elaine**: Well I can't at the moment, I've got the kids to look after, I've got to get childcare so …

**Matthew**: That makes sense, yeah, you'll need some childcare. What would you have to do to arrange some childcare for a few hours?

**Elaine**: Well, I'm wondering maybe my sister could help. I could ask her I suppose. I don't know what she'll say.

**Matthew**: Nice idea Elaine. When do you think you'll ask her?

**Elaine**: Well, she's busy today, but I'll try and text her tonight.

**Matthew**: Try and text her tonight?

**Elaine**: I will text her tonight.

**Jamie**: How much childcare are you going to ask her for?

**Elaine**: I could ask for a couple of mornings or afternoons each week; I don't know what she'll say though.

**Matthew**: Well, that's great, you're going to ask her – brilliant. And when do you think you'll get to the Jobcentre?

**Elaine**: I'm a bit busy this week, but I reckon I'm free on Thursday – I'll go then. Maybe Gill could help then?

**Matthew**: Gill?

**Elaine**: My sister.

**Matthew**: Well that sounds like a plan. Hey, let me just summarise: you're going to text your sister tonight to arrange some childcare, you're going to go down to the Jobcentre and get a CV written, and then you're going to start applying for jobs – is that right?

**Elaine**: Yeah, that's what I'm going to do.

**Matthew**: I need to check something with you Elaine: are you serious about this?

**Elaine**: What do you mean?

**Matthew**: About going to the Jobcentre, asking your sister, applying for jobs.

**Elaine**: Well of course I'm serious about it.

**Matthew**: Ok, and remind me why are you going to do this? What will it do for you?

**Elaine**: I really, really need to do something. My life is such a mess, something's got to change.

**Matthew**: And how will this help?

**Elaine**: Well it's a starting point, isn't it?

**Matthew**: And how will feel when you're holding down a job, do you think?

**Elaine**: Good. Yeah, proud. You know, feel like I'm doing something.

**Matthew**: Doing something about what exactly?

**Elaine**: About looking after my family, you know, a wage. Like I said, it's a starting point isn't it.

**Matthew**: It is Elaine, it really is. So if I text you on Thursday, what are you going to be able to tell me?

**Elaine**: Hopefully …

**Matthew**: Hopefully?

**Elaine**: Well, you know, how I got on at the Jobcentre, CV and that … and with Gill, you know, looking after the kids for a couple of days.

**Matthew**: You really do have a plan don't you!

**Elaine**: Yeah, I have.

## Example 3: High street retail – managing price differentials

Richard works as a sales and service consultant for a high street retailer. His job role is to help customers take advantage of the excellent service proposition his company offers.

The challenge he is wrestling with is the price differential between his company brand and lower prices offered by competitors. This has affected his confidence as a sales and service professional and also his performance measures. Alice is helping him think through how he can regain his confidence and get his performance back where it belongs.

**Alice**: Ok Richard, so there's something playing on your mind a little bit at the moment, that's maybe causing you some difficulty. Tell me about that.

**Richard**: So yeah, it's around pricing and when, with a customer, our price, bundle price, is coming in slightly higher than the competition's. I just don't have much confidence in delivering that price and yeah, my numbers are falling a bit.

**Alice**: Competitors are lower priced?

**Richard**: Yeah, it's difficult to get round that one, it's a fact. I'm a bit stuck, I guess.

**Alice**: Yeah I understand, stuck. Ok, just stay with me for a moment, let's just imagine a future time when you are able to present those bundle prices with confidence – what would that do for you?

**Richard**: To be fair, the prices … you know, we're a premium product, the prices are not the cheapest – they are what they are.

**Alice**: I understand what you're saying.

**Richard**: I know what you're saying about being confident, but it's still the same price issue.

**Alice**: Well, I acknowledge that. Let's just hold on to that thought for a moment – we'll think about the how in a moment – let's just think of a future time. Pretend if you like that you are able to present, with confidence, the bundle package.

**Richard**: Yeah?

**Alice**: A package product that may be a little bit more expensive than competitors, but let's just imagine that you are able to present with confidence. What would that do for you?

**Richard**: Well … if …

**Alice**: If?

**Richard**: If I had that confidence to do it, I suppose it would help me to kind of overcome objections – related to price anyway – sort of more confidently and more frequently as well, I suppose.

**Alice**: Alright, what else would it do for you?

**Richard**: Well, if I do that then I suppose, in terms of my overall credibility with the customer, it would impact as well, because I've got more confidence, which ultimately will lead to more sales and hitting targets and overachieving.

**Alice**: Alright,what will that do for you?

**Richard**: It gives me a better wage package and commission – extra cash.

**Alice**: Whey! Yeah ... what you going to do with that?

**Richard**: Spoil my little girl rotten!

**Alice**: Spoil your little girl; you'd like that, right?

**Richard**: I'd love that.

**Alice**: Ok, alright ... hey, well let's just think this through, ok? Let's think it though. What would have to happen for you to be able to present with confidence about the bundle of products that's got a price differentiator? What would have to happen for you to feel that confidence?

**Richard**: I think ... I suppose I would have to understand the difference and why the difference is there, and the value and the benefit for the customer – and understand some of that, yeah.

**Alice**: That makes sense doesn't it?

**Richard**: Yeah.

**Alice**: Alright, so how would you go about doing that? What would have to happen for you to be able to have that understanding, that knowledge?

**Richard**: Well I could spend some time with the sales coach and work with them for a bit.

**Alice**: Yeah – makes sense doesn't it?

**Richard**: Yeah.

**Alice**: Hey, I know sometimes you have to wait a little while for the sales coach to come around, so what could you do in between now and then that would enable you to have that additional knowledge? What other options have you got?

**Richard**: I suppose I could spend some time with Rosalba, I suppose.

**Alice**: Is she good at this, is she?

**Richard**: Yeah, she's always successful; she's doing well, so yeah … I suppose I could spend some time with her.

**Alice**: Alright, ok … so Rosalba is talented at this?

**Richard**: Yes.

**Alice**: She presents with confidence?

**Richard**: She does. She overcomes those price objections a lot better than I can at the moment.

**Alice**: Alright, so it would be helpful for us to understand what it is Rosalba does and how she does it?

**Richard**: Yes.

**Alice**: Right ok, and you think that getting together with her might be a useful thing to do?

**Richard**: Yeah, I think if I can just shadow her for a bit.

**Alice**: Shadow her?

**Richard**: Shadow her for a bit, and then maybe then she can kind of observe me a little bit.

**Alice**: Alright … ok, so what do we need to do to enable that, to make that happen?

**Richard**: Well she's in tomorrow, so I can have a word with her tomorrow and get together and, you know, work with her a little bit – see what she's doing.

**Alice**: Alright … ok, and maybe do a bit of shadowing, look at what she does?

**Richard**: Yeah, just ask her a couple of questions and just kind of … just, I think seeing her do it will kind of give me a few hints and tips.

**Alice**: That sounds like a great plan doesn't it?

**Richard**: Yeah.

**Alice**: Ok so let me just summarise this: sometime tomorrow, what time specifically are you going to do this?

**Richard**: So, well … I know we're both here in the morning, and before that you know the mid-time rush, so eleven-ish.

**Alice**: Eleven-ish?

**Richard**: Eleven.

**Alice**: Ha ha! Eleven, alright cool. So 11 o'clock tomorrow morning you're going to get together with Rosalba – maybe not have the conversation in detail, but at least start the process of finding out how she does what she does so well and that will enable you to gain what?

**Richard**: Well, you know, get my knowledge up and my confidence up when I'm talking around the price. I can overcome the objection, and then deliver the price.

**Alice**: And to get that confidence what would you gain from Rosalba? What she does specifically, around what?

**Richard**: In terms of, well, how she sells the value and the benefits of the products, to overcome the price difference.

**Alice**: And that knowledge will give you the confidence you need?

**Richard**: Yeah, I think so. Yeah, I just need to know it, that's all.

**Alice**: To be able to do what?

**Richard**: To be able to sell the value and benefit.

**Alice**: Alright ok … and remind me, what will that do for you?

**Richard**: Well, other than give me the confidence, it's going to help with my credibility, help me overcome objections as well, which is massive, so yeah.

**Alice**: What's that going to lead to?

**Richard**: That's going to help me achieve … and overachieve my target.

**Alice**: Alright!

**Richard**: Which is brilliant – which leads to more money!

**Alice**: And what are you going to do with the money?

**Richard**: Spoil my daughter.

**Alice**: That's something that's important to you right?

**Richard**: Oh, massively, yeah.

**Alice**: Ok then … hey, let me just check something: is this something you're definitely going to do?

**Richard**: Yeah

**Alice**: What? Tomorrow morning at 11?

**Richard**: Yeah … 11 o'clock.

**Alice**: Ok … hey, if I give you a call tomorrow afternoon, just to find out about how you got on with Rosalba, would that be a good thing to do?

**Richard**: Yeah absolutely. Although with my new skills I'll be busy with customers, obviously! I'll have to call you back!

**Alice**: Ha ha! Fantastic Richard. Alright, good luck in all that.

**Richard**: Thank you. Speak to you tomorrow.

## Example 4: Automotive aftersales – service care plans

Andrea is a service adviser at a large automotive dealership group. Service advisers work in the aftersales division of most major manufacturers' network of retail dealerships. A key role of the service adviser is to provide a professional service and maintenance experience for car owners and users. Car servicing, annual tests, repairs, manufacturer's original equipment parts and accessories form part of a comprehensive range of service propositions available to customers.

Included within the aftersales range are service care plans, an opportunity for customers to spread servicing costs over a full year, often interest-free. Customers can feel comfortable knowing their annual service costs are already covered (in most cases) by a simple monthly fee. Customers benefit from a plan designed around their specific driving habits and needs, and often include a roadside assistance package included in the service plan.

Andrea has a limiting belief about her ability to introduce service plans to her customers. This is inhibiting her performance in the business and is restricting the opportunities for customers to access the full range of services available from this main dealer. Andrea has a mindset that she 'just can't do it'.

Matt – Andrea's team leader – is helping her to break through her restrictive thinking patterns using Can't to Can Belief Busting. The initial conversation explores the internal 'frame' Andrea has placed around the introduction of service plans to customers and the differential impact of thinking about *helping* rather than *selling*.

The discussion also identifies some uncertainties in Andrea's mind about how to go about introducing the benefits of service plans. Her knowledge base is weak, and this is hampering her confidence.

**Matt**: Ok, so tell me what's happening with service plans?

**Andrea**: I can't do it. I've tried – I just can't. I'm no good at selling – it's not me.

**Matt**: Ok. What do you like doing?

**Andrea**: What do you mean?

**Matt**: Well, what do you like about your job? What's good about it?

**Andrea**: Helping customers. I like helping customers.

**Matt**: Ok, so do service plans help customers?

**Andrea**: Yes, obviously.

**Matt**: Ok. So, if you could help customers by introducing and explaining how service plans might help them, would that be good?

**Andrea**: Well, yeah, hadn't thought about it like that.

**Matt**: Helping customers is what we're about. We're not here to sell. You ok with that?

**Andrea**: Well, yes.

**Matt**: Hey, we can still help customers to buy our services, though, services that add value for them. If we don't let them know about how we can help them, that wouldn't be very good would it?

**Andrea**: Yeah, right, of course.

**Matt**: Ok, so let's start again, tell me about introducing service plans, helping customers to use our services.

**Andrea**: I'm just not very good at the new service plans, I don't feel confident. I don't really know how to set it up, well … I just don't know how it all works really, you know, when I'm talking to customers. I've tried … I just get nervous and I've messed it up a couple of times. I don't really know what I'm doing Matt, I can't get to grips with it. I can't do it.

**Matt**: Ok, getting to grips with it.

**Andrea**: I can't do it; I have a complete mental block and I know I avoid service plans because I'm worried I'm going to mess it up.

**Matt**: Well, ok, got that … so, what would happen if you could add real value for customers by introducing service plans? Properly get to grips with it and be really good at it? Like *really* good? The best!

**Andrea**: Matt, I just find this difficult ok. I don't know.

**Matt**: Alright … hey, let's just imagine … alright, just imagine, pretend, sometime in the future – I don't know when, some future situation, for whatever reason – you've become really good at introducing service plans, I mean really good.

**Andrea**: What? Better than Colin?

**Matt**: Ha! Yes, better than Colin. What will that do for you? How would you feel? Helping customers with this fabulous service we can offer.

**Andrea**: Ha! Right. Well, I'd get you off my back, and I'd feel good – like I'm doing what I'm supposed to be doing.

**Matt**: And what else?

**Andrea**: Well, like you said earlier, that I'm helping customers and not selling.

**Matt**: Keep going, what else will it do? When you're really amazing at this introducing service plans.

**Andrea**: Er … well, customers will get great service from us and I'd feel good about that.

**Matt**: Good? In what way, 'good'? What will the feeling be for you?

**Andrea**: Like satisfaction, sort of feeling professional, satisfaction, that kind of thing.

**Matt**: Oh, ok. Cool. And would you like that? Would you like those feelings?

**Andrea**: Yeah, of course I would.

**Matt**: Well alright then, so what would have to happen for you to be able to do that?

**Andrea**: Like I said, confidence – I'd need to feel more confident.

**Matt**: That's fair enough, isn't it? So what would have to happen for you to feel more confident, do you think?

**Andrea**: I'd need to know more about it. I wasn't there on the training day and the e-learning thing won't be ready for another few weeks apparently, Colin was telling me. I don't like e-learning anyway.

**Matt**: Ok Andrea, so how can you go about gaining the extra knowledge that you'd like to have?

**Andrea**: I could have some more training. I don't know if there's going to be any more?

**Matt**: None planned. What other options do you have?

**Andrea**: I could ask Colin to take me through it. He's really good at service plans.

**Matt**: You can be good at service plans too, even better than Colin. It's a good idea though. How could you go about asking him?

**Andrea**: I'll just ask him.

**Matt**: Ok, good. When will that be, do you think?

**Andrea**: When he's back in on Monday.

**Matt**: Excellent. What time?

**Andrea**: Oh I don't know! 7.30, when he comes in. I'll make him a cuppa!

**Matt**: Smart move. What else will you need?

**Andrea**: What do you mean?

**Matt**: Training materials? The training slides? Latest version?

**Andrea**: Oh yeah, that'd be good. Can I get them from training?

**Matt**: I would have thought so. How are you going to get them?

**Andrea**: I suppose I could email them.

**Matt**: Ok, and when will you do that?

**Andrea**: I'll do it this afternoon, when I'm back at my desk.

**Matt**: Oh yeah? [teasing grin] What time specifically Andrea? There's no escape!

**Andrea**: Ha! Alright. 2.30 on the dot I will email the training guys and get the slides.

**Matt**: Nice. Ok, so let's just check what you've told me: on Monday, at 7.30, when Colin comes back in, you're going to make him a cuppa and ask for some time with him so he can explain how he goes about helping customers by introducing service plans, is that right?

**Andrea**: Yep.

**Matt**: And in the meantime you're going to contact training – let me see if I've got this right – at 2.30 this afternoon … ha ha! … and you're going to ask them to email over the latest version of the training slides about service plans – right so far?

**Andrea**: Yep.

**Matt**: And this will give you the knowledge you've been missing, and do what for you?

**Andrea**: Give me confidence.

**Matt**: To do what?

**Andrea**: To explain service plans to customers, to help them with their service costs, spread over the year, helping them – not selling to them.

**Matt**: And to do it really well, right? Even better than Colin!

**Andrea**: I wish! Yeah. Ok, yeah … to do it really well.

**Matt**: Alright … and how's that going to make you feel? To be able to do that *really* well?

**Andrea**: Good, confident, that I'm helping customers, being professional.

**Matt**: You said about feeling satis… [pause]

**Andrea**: Yeah, satisfaction from doing a good job. Yeah, and keeping you off my back!

**Matt**: And keeping me off your back, yes … that's true. And you'd like those feelings, would you? Confidence, feeling you're really helping customers, satisfied, a sense of being pro…

**Andrea**: [Interrupts] Professional.

**Matt**: Yeah, and you'd like those feelings would you?

**Andrea**: Yes, I would.

**Matt**: Alright. So is this something you're going to do? Your plan for making it happen?

**Andrea**: Yes, I am going to do it.

**Matt**: Really?

**Andrea**: Yes, really. I'll go and send that email now.

**Matt**: Excellent. So, when shall we catch up to find out how you're getting on with your new skills?

**Andrea**: Middle of next week, after I've spent time with Colin.

**Matt**: Good plan Andrea. How about Thursday 3 p.m., before the rush? Let's meet here in the boardroom again.

**Andrea**: Ok. Plan.

**Matt**: Nice one Andrea, it's in my diary.

**Andrea**: And mine; don't worry!

## Example 5: Call centre operations – solving technical difficulties for customers

Megan works as a customer service agent in a large call centre. Her calls are inbound from customers relating to telephone and internet services. Some customer calls are about technical issues and she is expected to have a good working knowledge of these. Sally – an internal coach – is helping her through a difficulty Megan has been experiencing recently.

Some terminology worth understanding:

- **Resolution**: solving the customer's query.
- **First time resolution**: solving the customer's query without the customer calling back.
- **Metrics**: a series of measures against which call centre agents' performance is measured.

**Sally**: Ok Megan, so there's something playing on your mind at the moment. Tell me about that.

**Megan**: It's around the limitations of a customer's network, it's having a conversation with them and explaining it's a limitation and delivering what might be annoying news to the customer. And it's just – I'm not grasping it at the moment. I'm not getting it at all. I feel uncomfortable about that …

**Sally**: Uncomfortable? Yeah, ok.

**Megan**: It's not being able to just deliver that information. I'm just finding it – it feels a bit difficult.

**Sally**: Feels a bit difficult? Alright, ok, I understand that. Hey, what would happen if you could have those conversations, comfortably, with customers?

**Megan**: To be honest I'm not really sure. I've tried to have the conversations, and it just doesn't seem to be happening, so I just don't think I can. I don't think it's possible to have one.

**Sally**: Ok, well … bear with me a moment. Let's just imagine some future time when you *are* able to have those conversations with real confidence. Just imagine that for a moment – some future space and time where you are able to do it really well – what would happen if you could have those conversations?

**Megan**: I mean, if I could have those conversations, it would give the customer confidence in what I'm telling them; it would give me confidence delivering that message to them. It's just going to be a benefit all round, for myself and the customer, being able to give them that confidence, that confident resolution.

**Sally**: Ok, and what would it do for you personally?

**Megan**: For me personally? I mean if I could deliver that confident message, then it would give me a better resolution rate for the customers, so …

**Sally**: Alright … ok … [nodding]

**Megan**: A better resolution rate would mean I'm hitting targets for all of my metrics, and then better metrics would then obviously lead me to achieving my bonus.

**Sally**: Oh! Bonus!

**Megan**: Yeah, which obviously means extra money.

**Sally**: What are you going to do with the extra money?

**Megan**: So, me and my partner are actually thinking about travelling to Thailand soon, so it would be amazing to have that little bit of extra bonus … so …

**Sally**: Oh wow! How about that? That would be fantastic wouldn't it?

**Megan**: It would be amazing!

**Sally**: Yeah, alright. Hey, well … would you like that?

**Megan**: Of course I would, so would he … absolutely love it.

**Sally**: Of course you would, so let's just think about this – what would have to happen for you to be able to have those confident conversations about the kind of things you've just discussed? What would have to happen for you to be able to do that?

**Megan**: So, in order to have that conversation around the limitations, we offer them the extender kit. It's really cool – so I've been told anyway – but I don't really know, you know, much about it.

**Sally**: Ok.

**Megan**: So, I'm not 100 per cent on that one piece of equipment, so I need to know more about that, have a bit more confidence in that piece of equipment.

**Sally**: Ok yeah, yeah I understand.

**Megan**: Before I can deliver that message.

**Sally**: Yeah, before delivering that message.

**Megan**: Rather than talking about something I don't know a great deal about.

**Sally**: Alright, well that makes sense doesn't it?

**Megan**: Yeah.

**Sally**: Ok, hey … so what could you do? What would have to happen for you to be able to have that confidence, to have that knowledge?

**Megan**: So I need to get a bit more information like you say, knowledge around the products. So one of the things maybe to understand it a bit better, I could get some training or look at shadowing a member of my team.

**Sally**: Oh ok, yeah. Other options?

**Megan**: Yeah, well, there's an online course, so I could maybe look at that – e-learning modules. Another one is a member of my team, Tom; he's got quite a bit of information about the extender kits – he seems quite savvy with them – so I could maybe spend some time with him and get a bit of learning for myself. And another option, just generally searching the internet finding out about the product, finding out what they do, how they work.

**Sally**: Ok.

**Megan**: Just a bit of research on them.

**Sally**: So you've got some choices there Megan.

**Megan**: Yeah, absolutely.

**Sally**: E-learning? Er … what was your colleague's name?

**Megan**: So, my colleague's name is Tom, on my team, he knows quite a lot.

**Sally**: He's good on this is he?

**Megan**: Yeah – he's amazing.

**Sally**: And the third option was internet search. So which of those three feels right for you?

**Megan**: Probably spending some time with Tom. I know him quite well; he's on my team so I would be able to learn from him quite easily. So probably that's going to be the easiest option for me.

**Sally**: The easiest option for you personally. Ok, alright … so I guess there's some time involved here. This whole operation is very time efficient, you're going to need to ring-fence some time.

**Megan**: Yeah …

**Sally**: So what would have to happen for you to be able to get that time with Tom?

**Megan**: So the best option for me would probably be … is to speak to my manager, see if we can get sometime booked in, and then maybe she could organise for an hour or two where we can go through that information and be able to do it.

**Sally**: Yeah, that sounds like a really good idea. Ok, so let's just follow this through: so what has to happen for you to have this conversation with your manager? When are you going to do that?

**Megan**: So my manager's in a meeting at the moment but she's due out about 3 o'clock so …

**Sally**: Today?

**Megan**: Yeah today, so as soon as I catch her today at 3 I'll be able to have that conversation and see if she can get us some time booked in.

**Sally**: Wow, how about that! So let's just run backwards from that then – so let's see if I got this right: 3 o'clock when your manager comes out of a meeting you're going to have a conversation with her to see if you can find some time for you and Tom to spend together.

**Megan**: Yeah.

**Sally**: About this particular set of knowledge that you know he's skilled at.

**Megan**: Yeah.

**Sally**: To transfer the technology to you. And what will that do for you?

**Megan**: So as soon as I get that information it's going to make my calls a lot easier.

**Sally**: Alright …

**Megan**: Give me confidence in delivering that message to the customer.

**Sally**: Yeah ...

**Megan**: And obviously delivering that message more confidently gives me a better resolution, so you know it will help my metrics to be achieved, and then from my metrics being achieved I'll be able to get my bonus.

**Sally**: Your bonus. And what are you going to do with the bonus?

**Megan**: Travel to Thailand.

**Sally**: Travel to Thailand! And you'd like to do that?

**Megan**: Yeah absolutely – it's something me and my partner really want to do.

**Sally**: Ok, alright ... I think we've got a plan here haven't we? I just need to check: is this something that you are definitely going to do? Or are you just thinking about it?

**Megan**: Absolutely, definitely going to do it – as soon as my manager comes out at 3 o'clock.

**Sally**: Well hey, look – how about I give you a call a bit later on at 5 or 6 or something like that? We can find out how you got on with that conversation and make sure we keep the momentum going. Would you be up for that?

**Megan**: Yeah, that would be great.

**Sally**: I think we've got a plan haven't we?

**Megan**: Yeah, feels good!

**Sally**: Yay ... feels good to me too. Well done Megan!

**Megan**: Brilliant, thank you.

**Sally**: You're welcome. Chat later.

# appendix 1: example action plans

# Family Nurturing

| Continue & Begin Fast Coaching Action Plan | |
|---|---|
| **Dad** | **Family (Dad's action plan)** |
| *continue to* | Help children cook once a week |
| *continue to* | Go to spin class with daughter once a week |
| *continue to* | 121 with each child once a month |
| *continue to* | Have Sunday dinner together |
| *continue to* | Dad and sons sport event each year |
| *continue to* | Date night with partner once a month |
| **Celebrate this!** | |
| *begin to* 1 | Read to youngest twice a week |
| What has to happen? | Decide which nights and ring-fence time |
| *begin to* 2 | Visit Mum every 2 weeks |
| What has to happen? | Diarise and agree with Mum. Meet Mum tonight |
| *begin to* 3 | Email or text sister once a month |
| What has to happen? | Outlook reminders – plug in 6 p.m. tonight |
| *Commitment is doing the thing you said you would do, long after the mood you said it in has left you!* | |
| Review date: | |

# Managing Domestic Finances

| Continue & Begin Fast Coaching Action Plan | |
|---|---|
| **Alice** | **Domestic Finance and Money** |
| *continue to* | Monthly budget for everything |
| *continue to* | Keep credit card below £200 pcm |
| *continue to* | Save £100 pcm for hols |
| *continue to* | Direct debit all bills |
| *continue to* | Check online accounts weekly |
| *continue to* | Put overtime pay in savings account |
| **Celebrate this!** | |
| *begin to* 1 | Review energy supplier |
| What has to happen? | Diarise 2-hour slot to research online |
| *begin to* 2 | Change mobile phone plan |
| What has to happen? | Call phone company tonight 6 p.m. |
| *begin to* 3 | Start a pension plan |
| What has to happen? | Arrange meeting this week with finance adviser |
| *Commitment is doing the thing you said you would do, long after the mood you said it in has left you!* | |
| Review date: | |

# Developing Retail Selling Skills

| Continue & Begin Fast Coaching Action Plan | |
| --- | --- |
| **Anushka** | **Retail Selling Skills** |
| *continue to* | Follow (most of) the sales process |
| *continue to* | Approach customers within 2 mins |
| *continue to* | Use 'truisms' to build rapport |
| *continue to* | Ask 2+ open questions |
| *continue to* | Demonstrate solutions specific to need and want |
| *continue to* | Use ABC and trial closes |
| **Celebrate this!** | |
| *begin to* 1 | Explain benefits as well as features |
| What has to happen? | Read up on *Meerkat Selling* book |
| *begin to* 2 | Summarise the discussion |
| What has to happen? | Make it habit, starting with next customer |
| *begin to* 3 | Ask for the order |
| What has to happen? | Know I've used sales process and be confident to ask |
| *Commitment is doing the thing you said you would do, long after the mood you said it in has left you!* | |
| Review date: | |

# Personal Health and Well-Being

| Continue & Begin Fast Coaching Action Plan | |
|---|---|
| **Tomasz** | **Health and Well-being** |
| *continue to* | Jog twice a week |
| *continue to* | No red meat, dairy or fried food |
| *continue to* | Glucosamine tablets every day for joints |
| *continue to* | 6-monthly cholesterol check |
| *continue to* | Meditation on train commute |
| *continue to* | Dog walk Sunday mornings |
| **Celebrate this!** | |
| *begin to* 1 | Check saturated fat content on shop sarnies |
| What has to happen? | Make it a habit to check labels |
| *begin to* 2 | Cut to less than 10 alcohol units each week |
| What has to happen? | Keep diary of alcohol units for 4 weeks. 8 a.m. each morning |
| *begin to* 3 | 'No work' weekend once a month |
| What has to happen? | Diarise quarterly |
| *Commitment is doing the thing you said you would do, long after the mood you said it in has left you!* | |
| Review date: | |

# Parenting childcare (SIDS)

| Continue & Begin Fast Coaching Action Plan | |
|---|---|
| **Qingzhao** | **Parenting Prevention of Sudden Infant Death Syndrome (SIDS)** |
| *continue to* | Place baby in sleep bag at sleep time |
| *continue to* | Place baby on her back to sleep, feet at bottom of Moses basket |
| *continue to* | Keep home temperature between 18 to 20 centigrade |
| *continue to* | Keep personal smoking below 10 cigarettes per day |
| *continue to* | When baby has rolled onto her tummy, turn her onto her back again |
| *continue to* | - |
| **Celebrate this!** | |
| *begin to 1* | Tuck in sheets under baby's armpits, no higher |
| What has to happen? | Make habit |
| *begin to 2* | Be ready to move baby into her own cot at 6 months old. Already have second-hand cot. Buy new mattress |
| What has to happen? | Save up/find £20 for Ebay purchase of new cot mattress |
| *begin to 3* | Stop smoking altogether |
| What has to happen? | Decide to become a non-smoker from now on |
| *Commitment is doing the thing you said you would do, long after the mood you said it in has left you!* | |
| Review date: | |

# Retirement – Making the Most of Leisure Time

| Continue & Begin Fast Coaching Action Plan | |
| --- | --- |
| **Nilesh** | **Leisure** |
| *continue to* | Watch live rugby/cricket each weekend |
| *continue to* | Cycle ride weekly |
| *continue to* | Maintain my classic car |
| *continue to* | Walk dog to pub Fridays |
| *continue to* | Once a year holiday to USA |
| *continue to* | Keep garden in check |
| **Celebrate this!** | |
| *begin to* 1 | Read one novel each quarter |
| What has to happen? | Set up reminders on Outlook |
| *begin to* 2 | Arrange one motorbike trip each month April–Sept |
| What has to happen? | Diarise monthly |
| *begin to* 3 | Attend a cooking course/event |
| What has to happen? | Google, book tickets and diarise |
| *Commitment is doing the thing you said you would do, long after the mood you said it in has left you!* | |
| Review date: | |

# Sport – Hockey Team Player

| Continue & Begin Fast Coaching Action Plan | |
|---|---|
| **Tommy** | **Sport** |
| *continue to* | Attend Tues and Thurs training every week (on time) |
| *continue to* | Warm up and stretch before match |
| *continue to* | Eat carbs Fri night b4 match day |
| *continue to* | Cross trainer Sundays loosen up |
| *continue to* | Get in right pre-match mental state |
| *continue to* | 10k row machine every Weds eve |
| **Celebrate this!** | |
| *begin to 1* | Ask for coach opinion on my game (weekly) |
| What has to happen? | After-match review with coach 5 p.m. each week |
| *begin to 2* | Warm down properly after match |
| What has to happen? | Ask coach for help through encouragement |
| *begin to 3* | Get to home games 90mins b4 start |
| What has to happen? | Arrange Saturday a.m. childcare each week |
| *Commitment is doing the thing you said you would do, long after the mood you said it in has left you!* | |
| Review date: | |

# Housing (Supported Living)

| Continue & Begin Fast Coaching Action Plan | |
| --- | --- |
| **Charlotte** | **Housing** |
| *continue to* | Get up before 9 a.m. |
| *continue to* | Shower every morning |
| *continue to* | Wash own clothes with washing machine |
| *continue to* | Cook my own dinner on Mondays, Wednesdays, Fridays and Saturdays |
| *continue to* | Clean the bathroom and toilet on Sundays |
| *continue to* | Go to craft group on Tuesdays |
| **Celebrate this!** | |
| *begin to* 1 | Stick to my weekly budget |
| What has to happen? | Get help from Geoff to work it out |
| *begin to* 2 | Spend more time with other residents |
| What has to happen? | Make tea and coffee for people in the living room and chat with them |
| *begin to* 3 | - |
| What has to happen? | - |
| *Commitment is doing the thing you said you would do, long after the mood you said it in has left you!* | |
| Review date: | |

# Automotive Sales – Sales Process Compliance

| Continue & Begin Fast Coaching Action Plan | |
|---|---|
| **Susie** | **Sales Process** |
| *continue to* | Acknowledge customer, smile, stand up and walk towards customer, introduce myself by name, offer customer a seat and hot refreshment |
| *continue to* | Take customer's details, name, address, mobile, email |
| *continue to* | Ask 6 questions about customer's needs |
| *continue to* | Ask about part exchange |
| *continue to* | Ask about financing, explained finance is available |
| *continue to* | Static demo of vehicle |
| **Celebrate this!** | |
| *begin to* 1 | Tie back features and benefits to qualification information |
| What has to happen? | Listen carefully to customer answers. Don't allow myself to rush. My personal discipline |
| *begin to* 2 | Offer an immediate test drive, or book a further appointment – not just say, 'We can arrange a test drive' |
| What has to happen? | Get my form of words right and practise |
| *begin to* 3 | Use trial closes throughout conversation |
| What has to happen? | Make it a habit |
| *Commitment is doing the thing you said you would do, long after the mood you said it in has left you!* | |
| Review date: | |

# appendix 2: sources of influence

The origins behind Continue & Begin Fast Coaching come from a diverse range of influences, including my own experiential learning and trial and error testing of hypotheses.

There are influencing agents at work in Continue & Begin, some of which can be traced to 'change' disciplines. Other influencers include cases and circumstances where early manifestations of Continue & Begin Fast Coaching were used to create change in a person's work life, education, sports performance, social life or family environment. Continue & Begin evolved and adapted over time. A (very) small group of Continue & Begin Fast Coaching Master Trainers have underpinning knowledge and understanding of these influences. I have shared insights with them.

Some time ago I was helping a UK business develop their national field team of area managers (AMs). I worked one-to-one, developing personal goals, 'resistor-busting' strategies and their personal plans to discover new knowledge through reading.

We discussed useful reference points for their personal development. We explored Bateson, Bandler and Grinder, George Zalucki and the wonderful Frank Farrelly. One of the AMs asked me which sources of learning had contributed most to the evolution of Continue &

Begin Fast Coaching; I promised to compile an indicative list of key influencers.

So, for the inquisitive, the enquiring, the enthralled and the entranced, below are a few reference points to enjoy. Now, if you were to begin the process of reading and were to uncover new understanding along the way, well that would be fine.

- Alfred Adler: teleological goal setting;
- Gregory Bateson: *patterns which connect*;
- Aaron Beck: reframing;
- Eric Berne: transactional analysis/PAC;
- Noel Burch: competence/incompetence model;
- Noam Chomsky: transformational grammar basics;
- Epictetus: preframing, framing;
- Milton Erickson: presuppositions, embedded commands, indirect suggestions, metaphor, analogue marking (communicating without words), non-specificity;
- Frank Farrelly: provocative methods;
- John Grinder and Richard Bandler: NLP, META model, Milton model, modelling excellence;*
- Avy Joseph: our imagination;
- Alfred Korzybski: nominalisations;
- George Miller's Law 7+/-2;
- Michel de Montagne: worry;
- Frank Pucelik: 95% is smoke;
- Carl Rogers: get inside their world;
- Hermann Rorschach: perception;
- Dmitri Uznadze: *yes sets*;
- Hans Vaihinger: useful fictions, Act As If;
- George Zalucki: commitment mantra.

*Included here within the category of 'influences' is the field (or more accurately 'fields') of NLP. In Continue & Begin work, I use selected nuggets from NLP alongside other ingredients. NLP is an often misunderstood set of personal-change tools of which some may be helpful to a coachee. Unfortunately, there is also unhelpful mystique, misinformation and drama about what NLP is and how it can be used. At the heart of NLP is the original strategy, which was its first – and in my opinion, still most valuable – application: the process of modelling excellence. The development of the META model and identification of the Milton model are – in my opinion – close runners-up.

Be careful what you learn …

# appendix 3: train the trainer (TTT) programme

Grow-your-own Continue & Begin Fast Coaching internal trainers!

Continue & Begin lends itself to a TTT format, especially for roll-out across a national or international estate, for large healthcare or local authority organisations or for call centre operations.

TTT helps create an internal Continue & Begin training capability, creating a team of in-house licensed trainers of Continue & Begin Fast Coaching, accredited and skilled to create new fast coaches in their businesses.

## Licensed Trainers of Continue & Begin Fast Coaching TTT Programme

Continue & Begin Fast Coaching training technology is transferred to organisations, either through in-house L&D teams or, where L&D resources are limited, to operational management teams. The TTT programme offers choice too: a combination approach engaging both L&D practitioners and operational managers works really well. This provides sustainability and longevity for the programme allowing an internal team to run follow-up events for new Continue & Begin fast coaches and refresher sessions.

The TTT approach consists of a 3-day programme of professional development:

### Day 1 of 2: Training
Potential licensed trainers of Continue & Begin Fast Coaching learn and experience the training day as delegates. Delivery is by Nick Drake-Knight, the creator of Continue & Begin Fast Coaching, and includes the latest developments in Continue & Begin application.*

### Day 2 of 2 – Practice workshop day
New trainers gain the underpinning knowledge to understand and enable them to effectively deliver the Continue & Begin Fast Coaching skills programme to colleagues.

It is realistic to accommodate up to 25 participants on days 1 and 2 of each TTT.

### Day 3 – Assessment Days
Each Fast Coaching trainer is assessed during his/her first delivery by Nick Drake-Knight (or certified training provider under his supervision) to ensure effective delivery and integrity of learning content. Upon successful performance the new trainer is accredited as a licensed trainer of Continue & Begin Fast Coaching within their organisation for a fixed term.

Contact nick@ndk-group.com or call on +44(0)7870 904636 to create an internal Continue & Begin Fast Coaching training function in your organisation.

---

* Continue & Begin Fast Coaching continues to evolve.

# appendix 4: testimonials

We put huge resources into increasing the competencies of our salespeople. Sustainability at local level is a fundamental basis of success. Coaching is only possible using a workable model, and Continue & Begin is just that. Helping store owners and managers to help their salespeople has a massive potential to increase sales and is an area we continue to support, especially in these challenging retail times.

**Steve Devonshire, Training Manager UK and Benelux, Bang & Olufsen**

The simplicity of the Continue & Begin process enables our managers to deliver effective coaching live on the shop floor and directly after the training event. This means it loses none of its impact, ensures the coachee gets maximum benefit, and doesn't end up as a dusty theory that seemed like a good idea on a hazy training day but never gets used.

**Steve O'Neill, Learning and Development Manager, Steinhoff Group – Harveys Furniture**

Continue & Begin Fast Coaching has helped us improve the lives of hundreds of families. I highly recommend Continue & Begin to all professionals working with families and individuals in need of help.

**Zoryna O'Donnell, Strengthening Families Programme Lead**

We went about training-in our new, simple, 5-step selling model. Crucially, however, we spent as much if not more time with our managers training them on how to coach this in, using Continue & Begin. This sounds obvious, but we'd underinvested in training our managers in the past and fell into the classic mistake of not building up the consistency and sustainability of our approach. With our newly adopted Continue & Begin model, the standards of coaching-in a better sales performance using observed data and metrics is of primary importance.

**Mike Hawes, Director of Organisational Development, B&Q PLC**

Nick and his team have worked hard to ensure our internal trainers are comfortable and confident in the delivery of Continue & Begin. Enthusiasm and attention to detail has ensured we feel capable as a business to really make a difference using fast coaching. The positive impact Continue & Begin is having in Virgin Media is already shining through. Managers and coaches are focusing on a behavioural rather than a traditional technical approach. This is reaping great benefits. The support Nick and his team offer on an ongoing basis will ensure the impact the model is having will continue. Continue & Begin is part of our DNA now and long may that continue.

**Simon Connolly, Head of Training and Development, Virgin Media**

Continue & Begin is one of those training courses where you realise its potential usefulness almost straight away. I have been using the techniques since day one and have been recommending it to anyone who will listen.

**James Lucas, Personal Budgets Officer, Southern Housing Group**

Continue & Begin has offered us a unique platform to start building the essential people management skills to grow our business. The results achieved have been incredible, measured in behavioural changes across the whole workforce. The easy approach and simplicity with which the training is delivered made investing in this product worth every single penny. The return is tangible from day one. We now have a consolidated and competitive commercial advantage.

**Paolo Cimbri, EMEA Retail Operations Manager, Oakley Europe**

No matter what barriers were put up, I was able to break them down using Can't to Can and we were able to start making progress.

**Jackie Drake, Strengthening Families Key Worker**

# further reading

**Alfred Adler**: teleological goal setting

Adler, A. (1956) *The Individual Psychology of Alfred Adler.* New York, NY: Basic Books.


**Richard Bandler, John Grinder, Carmen Bostic St. Clair**: modelling excellence, fuzzy language, META model, Milton model, reframing, NLP (Neuro-Linguistic Programming)

Bandler, R. & Grinder, J. (1975) *The Structure of Magic Volume 1.* Palo Alto, CA: Science and Behaviour Books.

Bandler, R. & Grinder, J. (1976) *The Structure of Magic Volume 2.* Palo Alto, CA: Science and Behaviour Books.

Bandler, R. & Grinder, J. (1979) *Frogs into Princes.* Moab, UT: Real People Press.

Bandler, R. & Grinder, J. (1981) *Trance-formations.* Moab, UT: Real People Press.

Bandler, R. & Grinder, J. (1982) *Reframing: Neuro Linguistic Programming and the Transformation of Meaning.* Moab, UT: Real People Press.

Bostic St. Clair, C. & Grinder, J. (2001) *Whispering in the Wind.* Scotts Valley, CA: J & C Enterprises.

**Gregory Bateson**: patterns which connect

Bateson, G. (1972) *Steps to an Ecology of Mind*. Chicago, IL: The University of Chicago Press.

Bateson, G. (2002) *Mind and Nature: A Necessary Unity*, Cresskill, NJ: Hampton Press.

Charlton, N.G. (2008) *Understanding Gregory Bateson*. Albany, NY: State University of New York Press.


**Aaron Beck**: reframing, cognitive restructuring

Beck, A.T. (1979) *Cognitive Therapy and the Emotional Disorders*. London: Penguin.


**Eric Berne**: transactional analysis, assertion

Berne, E. (1964) *Games People Play: The Psychology of Human Relationships*. London: Penguin.


**Richard Boyatzis** *et al*: inspirational positive coaching

Boyatzis, R.E., Jack, A.I., Khawaja, M.S., Passarelli, A.M. & Leckie, R.L. (2013) *Visioning in the brain: an fMRI study of inspirational coaching and mentoring*. Department of Cognitive Science, Case Western Reserve University, Cleveland, OH.


**Noel Burch/Gordon Training International**: competence/incompetence model

http://www.gordontraining.com/free-workplace-articles/learning-a-new-skill-is-easier-said-than-done/


**Noam Chomsky**: transformational grammar basics, surface structure, deep structure

Chomsky, N. (1965) *Aspects of the Theory of Syntax*. Cambridge, MA: MIT Press.

**David Cohen**: body language, non-verbal communication

Cohen, D. (1992) *Body Language in Relationships*. London: Sheldon Press.

**Nick Drake-Knight**: (Old Code) Continue & Begin Fast Coaching in business-to-consumer retail customer service and sales, emotional drivers, chunking processes and behaviours

Drake-Knight, N. (2007) *Boomerang!* London: Pollinger Limited.

Drake-Knight, N. (2008) *Meerkat Selling*. London: Pollinger Limited.

**Albert Ellis**: disputing irrational beliefs

Ellis, A. & Dryden, W. (1999) *The Practice of Rational Emotive Behaviour Therapy*. London: Free Association Books.

Ellis, A. & MacLaren, C. (1998) *Rational Emotive Therapy: A Therapist's Guide*. Atascadero, CA: Impact Publishers.

**Epictetus**: pre-framing, framing

*The Enchiridion*, 135 ACE

**Milton Erickson**: presuppositions, embedded commands, indirect suggestions, metaphor, non-specificity, analogue marking (communicating through tone and non-verbal emphasis)

Battino, R. & South, T. (1999) *Ericksonian Approaches: A Comprehensive Manual*. Carmarthen, Wales: Crown House Publishing.

Bandler, R. & Grinder, J. (1975) *Patterns of the Hypnotic Techniques of Milton Erickson, M.D. Volume 1*. Scotts Valley, CA: Grinder & Associates.

Erickson, M.H. & Rosen, S. (1982) *My Voice Will Go with You*. London: W.W. Norton & Company.

Erickson, M.H., Rossi, E.L. & Rossi, S.I. (1976) *Hypnotic Realities: The Induction of Clinical Hypnosis and Forms of Indirect Suggestion*. Stratford, NH: Irvington Publishers.

**Frank Farrelly**: provocative methods, humour

Farrelly, F. & Brandsma, J.M. (1989) *Provocative Therapy*. Soquel, CA: Meta Publications.

**Robert Firestone, Lisa Firestone, Joyce Catlett**: critical inner voice

Firestone, R., Firestone, L. & Catlett, J. (2002) *Conquer Your Critical Inner Voice*. Oakland, CA: New Harbinger Publications.

**Judith Glaser, Richard Glaser**: positive conversations

Glaser, J.E. & Glaser, R.D. (2014) 'The Neurochemistry of Positive Conversations.' *Harvard Business Review*, June 12.

**David Gordon**: metaphors, stories, fables

Gordon, D. (1978) *Therapeutic Metaphors*. Cupertino, CA: META Publications.

**David Groves, Wendy Sullivan, Judy Rees**: clean language

Sullivan, W. & Rees, J. (2008) *Clean Language: Revealing Metaphors and Opening Minds*. Carmarthen, Wales: Crown House Publishing.

**Avy Joseph**: our imagination

London College of Clinical Hypnosis (2005) Diploma in Clinical Hypnosis, lecture content.

**Alfred Korzybski**: the map is not the territory, the menu is not the food, limitations of language to describe meaning, feeling and experience

Korzybski, A. (1933) *Science and Sanity: An Introduction to Non-Aristotelian Systems and General Semantics*, 5th edition (Jan. 1995). Forest Hills, NY: Institute of General Semantics.

**Brian Mayne**: goal mapping, life mapping

Mayne, B. & Mayne, S. (2002) *Life Mapping*. London: Vermillion.

Mayne, B. & Mayne, S. (2006) *Goal Mapping*. London: Watkins Publishing.

**Albert Mehrabian**: words, tone (song) and physiology (dance)
Mehrabian, A. (1971) *Silent Messages*. Belmont, CA: Wadsworth Publishing.

✍ **George Miller**: seven plus or minus two, working memory capacity, chunking information
Miller, G. (1956). 'The magical number seven, plus or minus two: Some limits on our capacity for processing information.' *The Psychological Review*, 63, 81–97.
McLeod, S.A. (2009). *Short Term Memory*. Retrieved from www. simplypsychology.org/short-term-memory.html

**Michel de Montaigne**: worry,
Michel de Montaigne (1580) *Essais*. Dordogne, France
http://www.gutenberg.org/files/3600/3600-h/3600-h.htm

**Desmond Morris**: body language, non-verbal communication
Morris, D. (1994) *Bodytalk: A World Guide to Gestures*. London: Johnathan Cape.

**Norman Vincent Peale**: positive thinking
Peale, N.V. (1953) *The Power of Positive Thinking*. London: Cedar.

**Frederick (Fritz) Perls**: personal responsibility for change
Perls, F.S. (1969) *In and Out the Garbage Pail*. Highland, NY: Real People Press.

**Frank Pucelik**: 95% is smoke
Grinder, J. & Pucelik, R.F. (2013) *The Origins of Neuro-Linguistic Programming*. Carmarthen, Wales: Crown House Publishing.
http://www.businessnlpacademy.co.uk/blog/view/frank_pucelik_on_ the_early_days_of_nlp/

**Anthony Robbins**: personal power, fulfilling potential.
Robbins, A. (1986) *Unlimited Power*. New York, NY: Simon & Schuster.

Robbins, A. (1991) *Awaken the Giant Within*. New York, NY: Simon & Schuster.

**Carl Rogers**: get inside their world
Rogers, C.R. (1980) *A Way of Being*. New York, NY: Houghton Mifflin Company.

**Virginia Satir**: positive intentions, words, body, insides, placating, blaming, computing, distracting, association and dissociation, challenging limiting beliefs, alternative choices, reframing, embedded commands, action
Satir, V. (1972) *Peoplemaking*. Palo Alto, CA: Science and behaviour Books.
Andreas, S. (1991) *Virginia Satir: The Patterns of Her Magic*. Moab, UT: Real People Press.

**Jonathan Sternfield**: firewalk, overcoming limiting beliefs
Sternfield, J. (1992) *Firewalk: The Psychology of Physical Immunity*. Stockbridge, MA: Berkshire House.

**Dmitri Uznadze**: Yes Sets and the regulation of thinking
Uznadze, D.N. (1966 translation) *The Psychology of Set*. The International Behavioral Sciences Series. New York, NY: Springer Science+Business.

**Hans Vaihinger**: useful fictions, Act As If
Vaihinger, H. (1925, translated from German, reprinted 2009) *The Philosophy of 'As If': A System of the Theoretical, Practical and Religious Fictions of Mankind*. Eastford, CT: Martino Publishing.

**Robert Anton Wilson**: domesticated primates
Wilson, R.A. (1983) *Prometheus Rising*. Las Vegas, NV: New Falcon Publications.

George Zalucki: commitment mantra
*Mind & Emotions* CD http://www.georgezalucki.com/

Be careful what you learn ...